This book belongs to

_____

Scan qr-code to leave a review

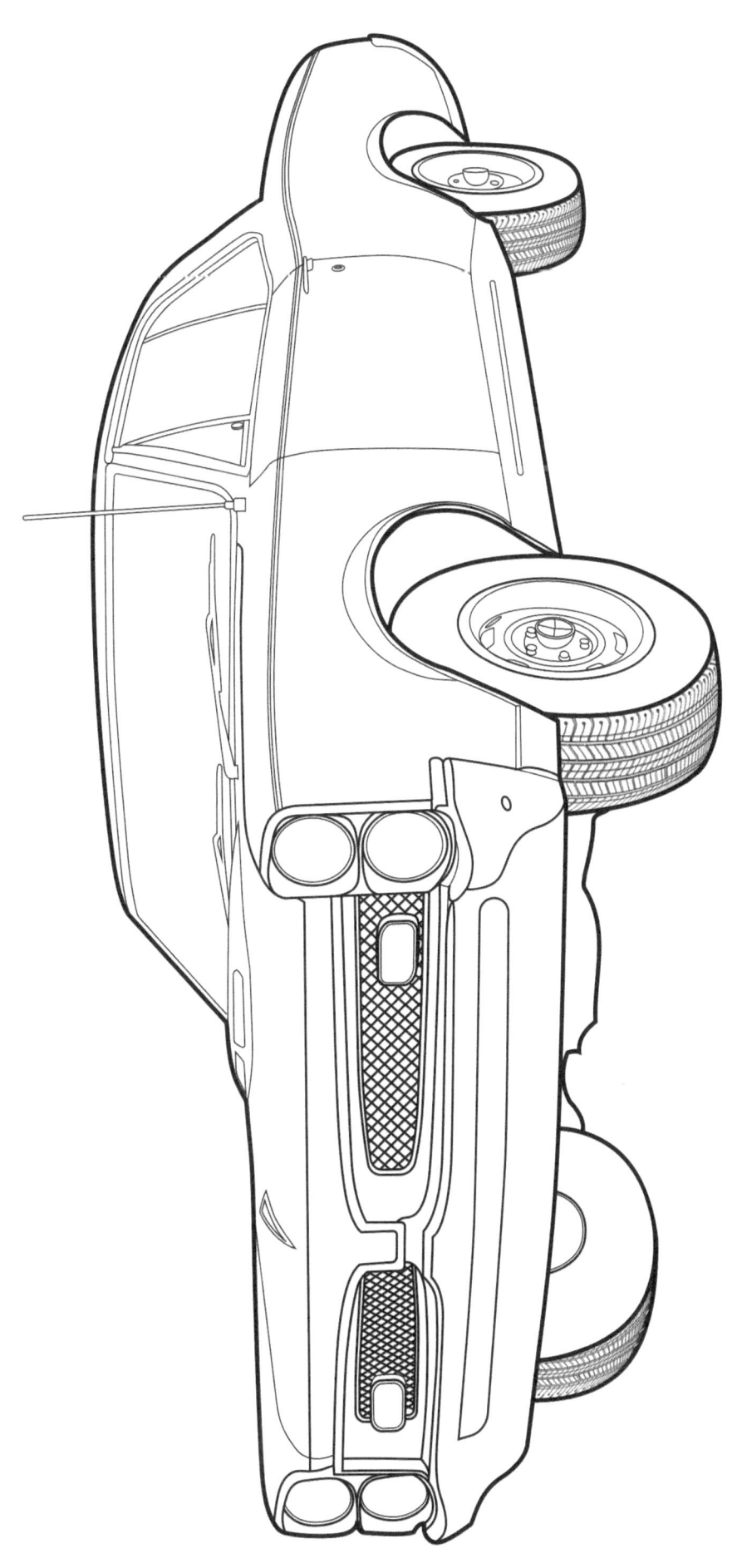

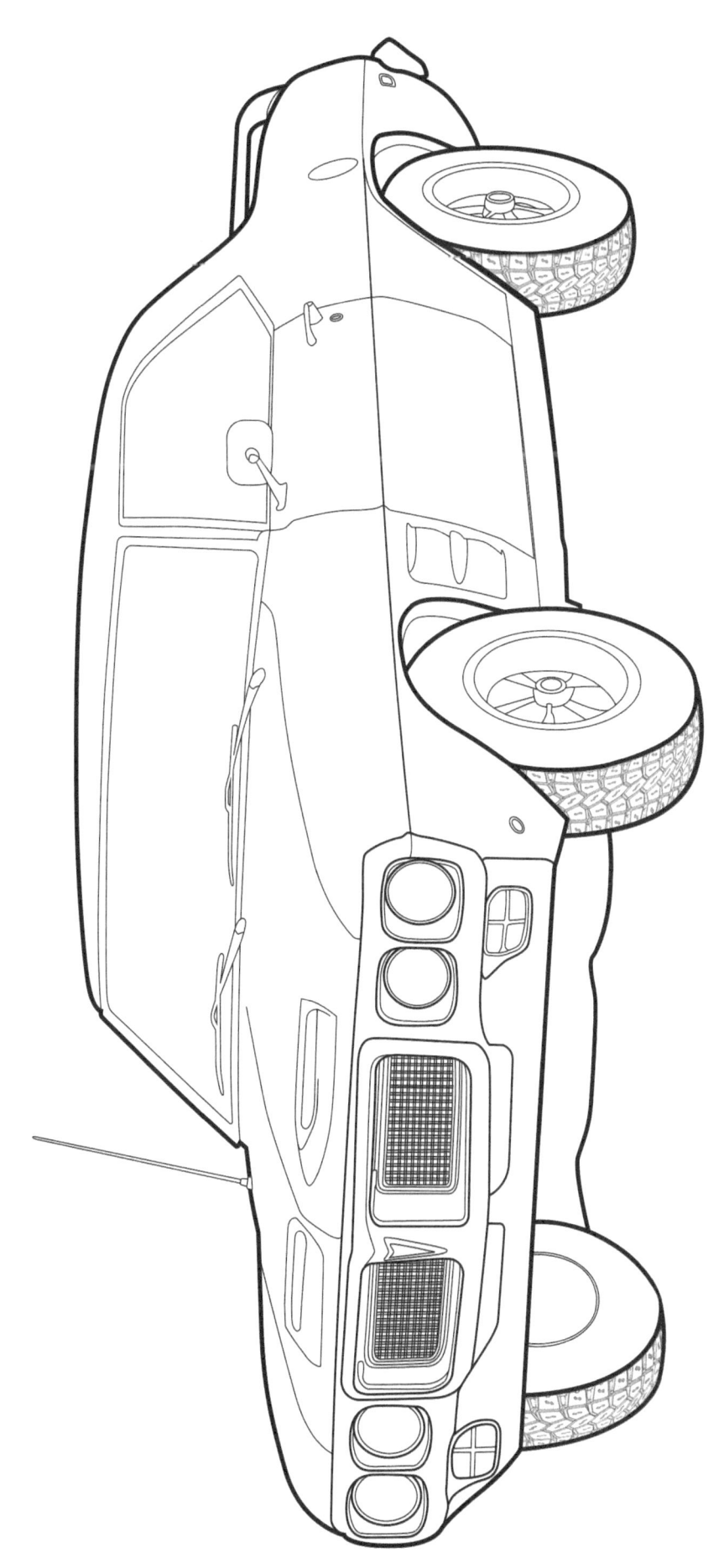

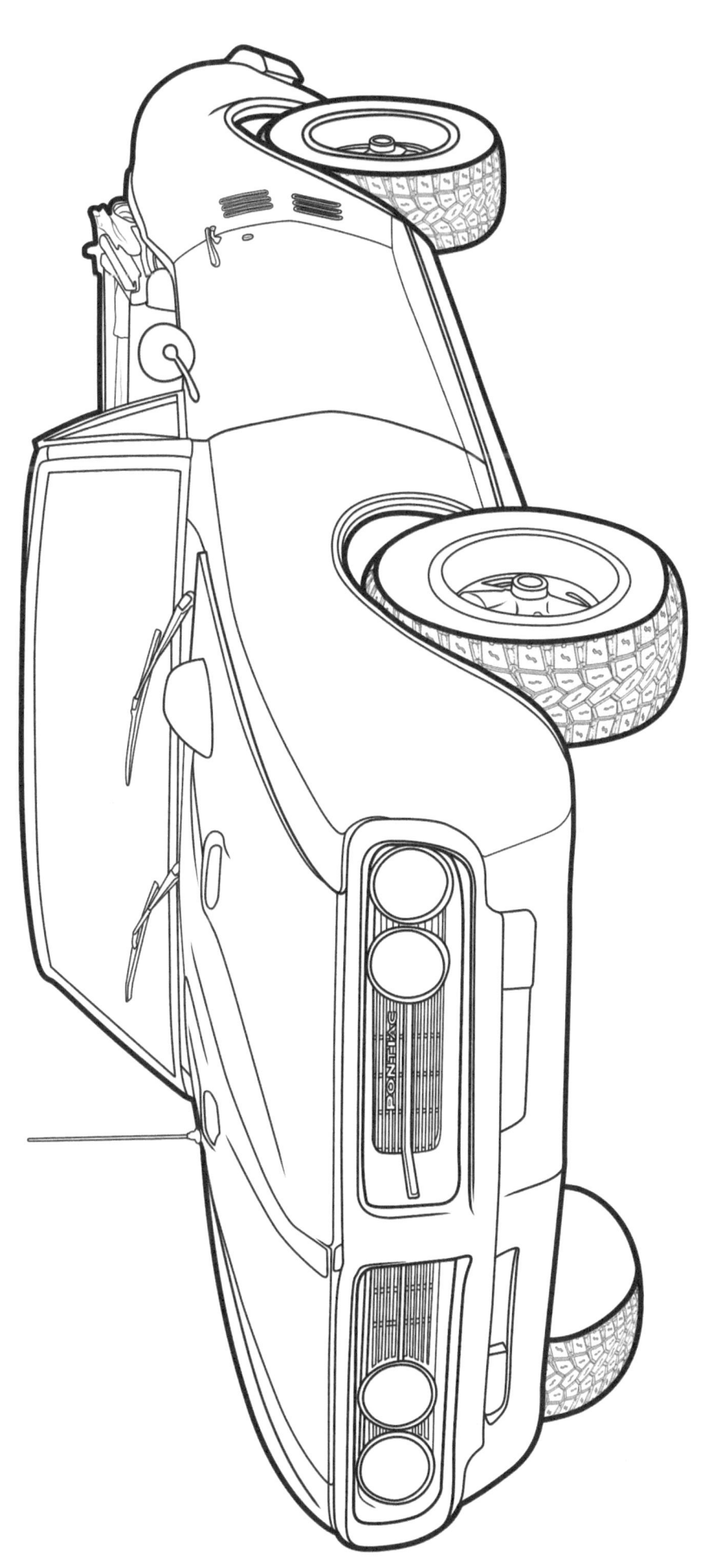

Pontiac Firebird 400 Convertible 1967

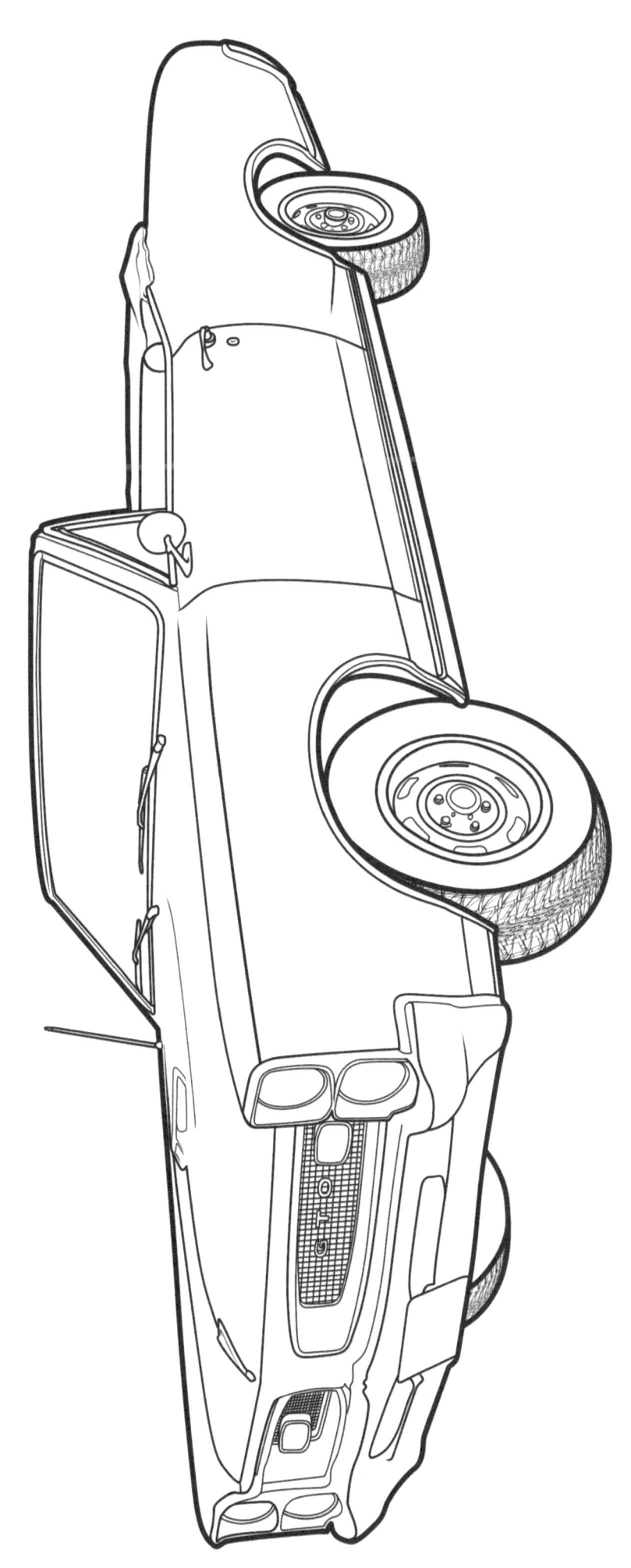

Pontiac GTO Judge Hardtop Coupe 1967

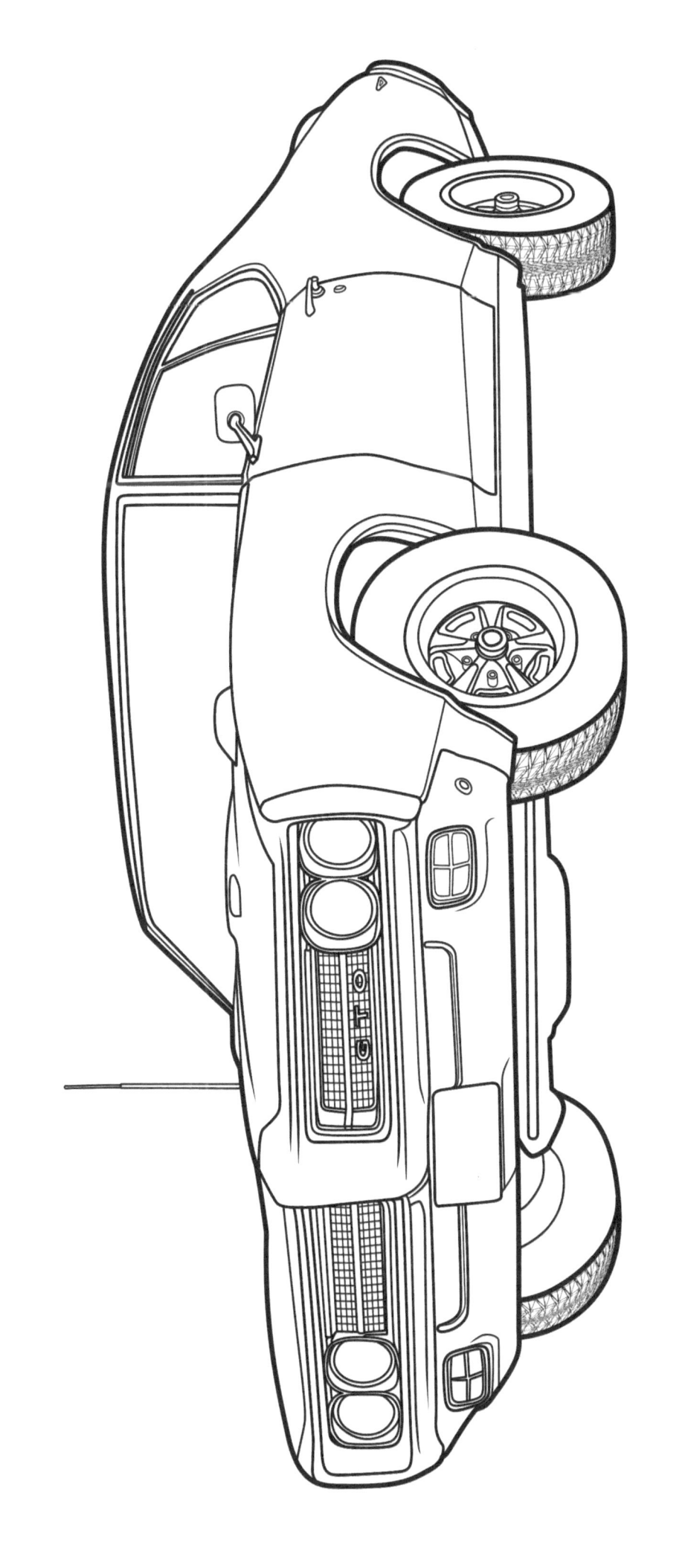

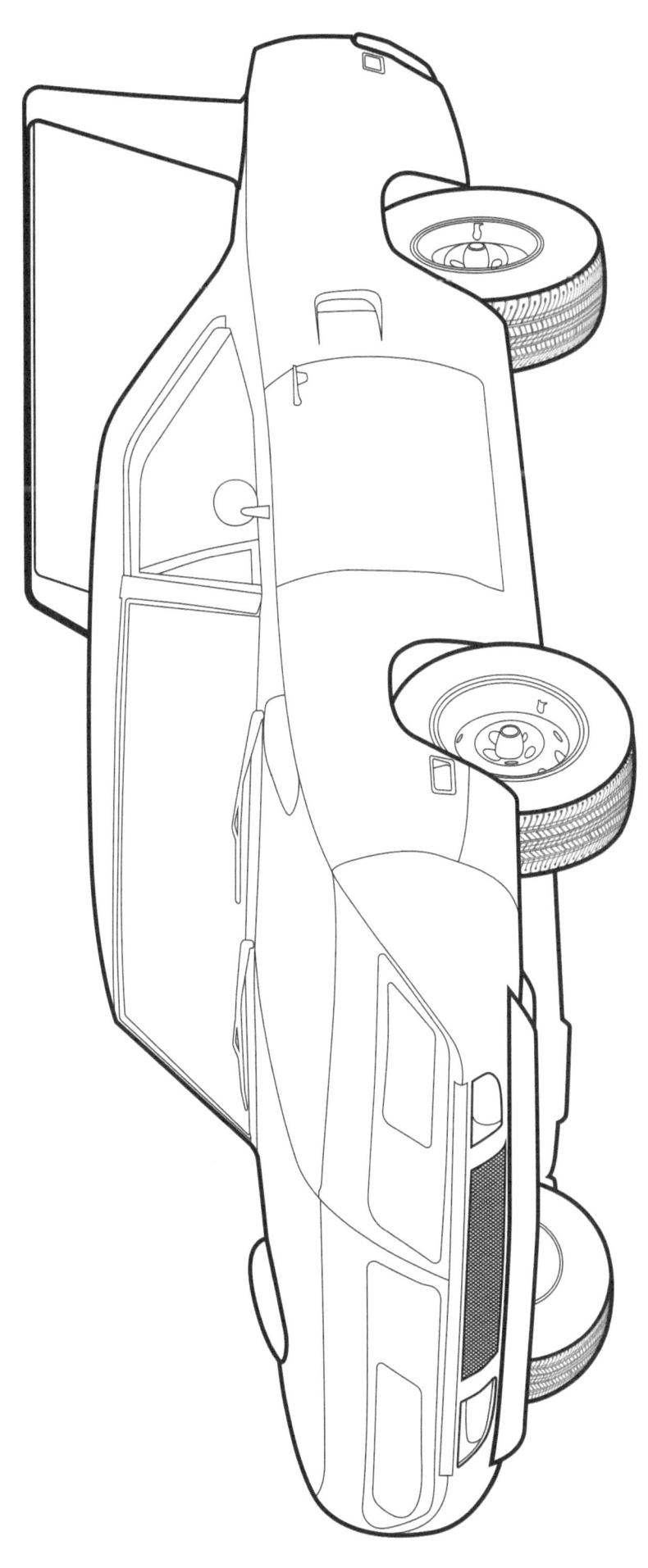

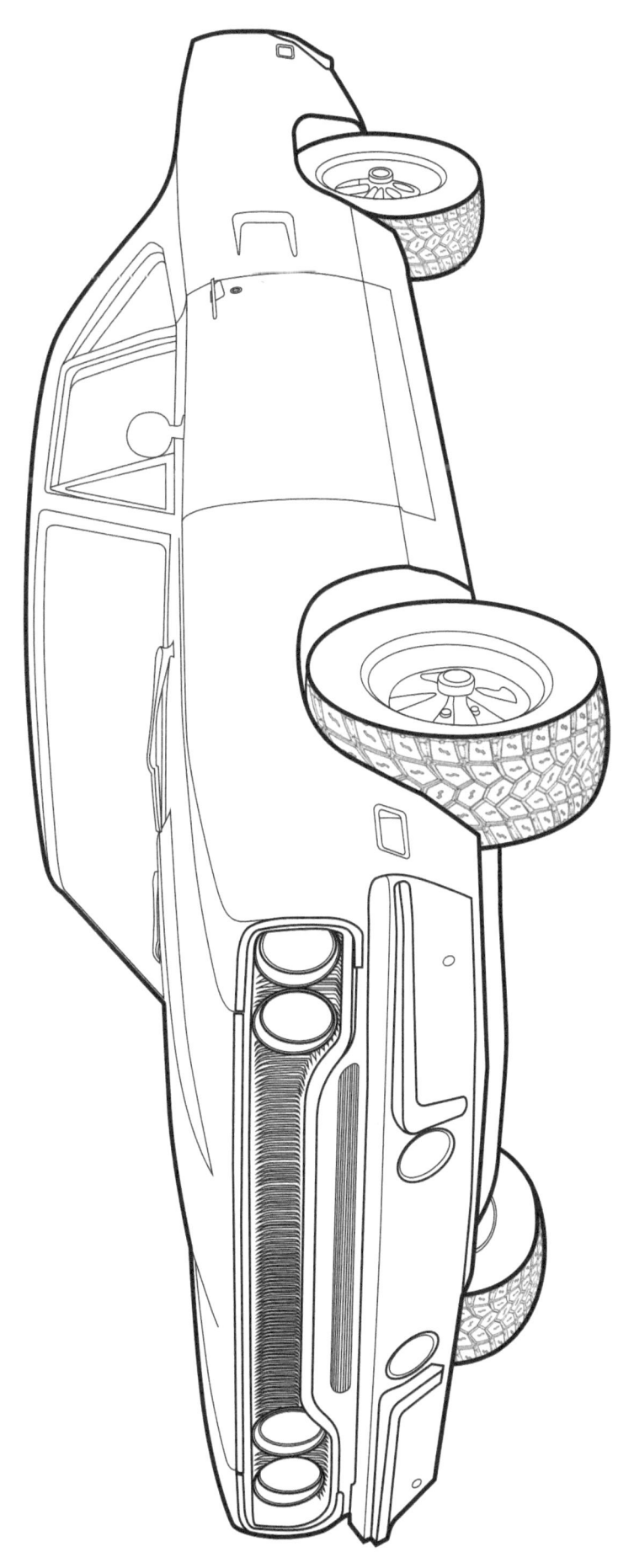

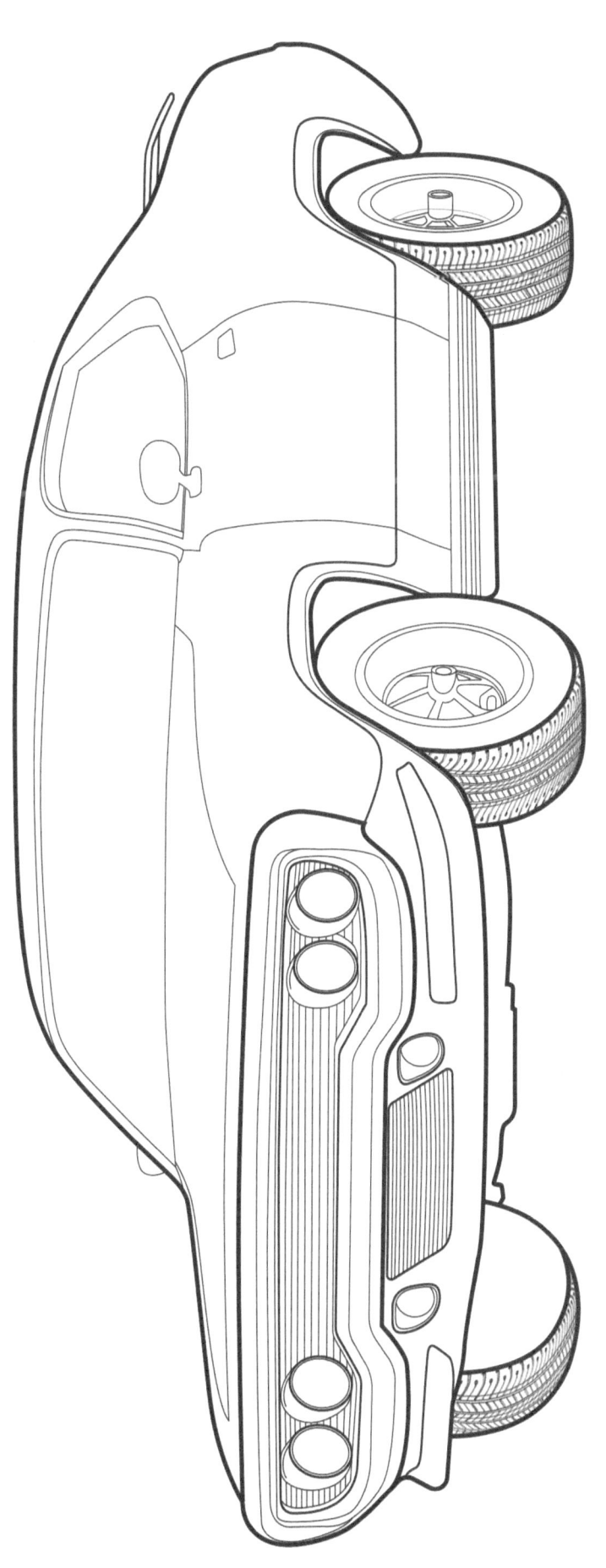

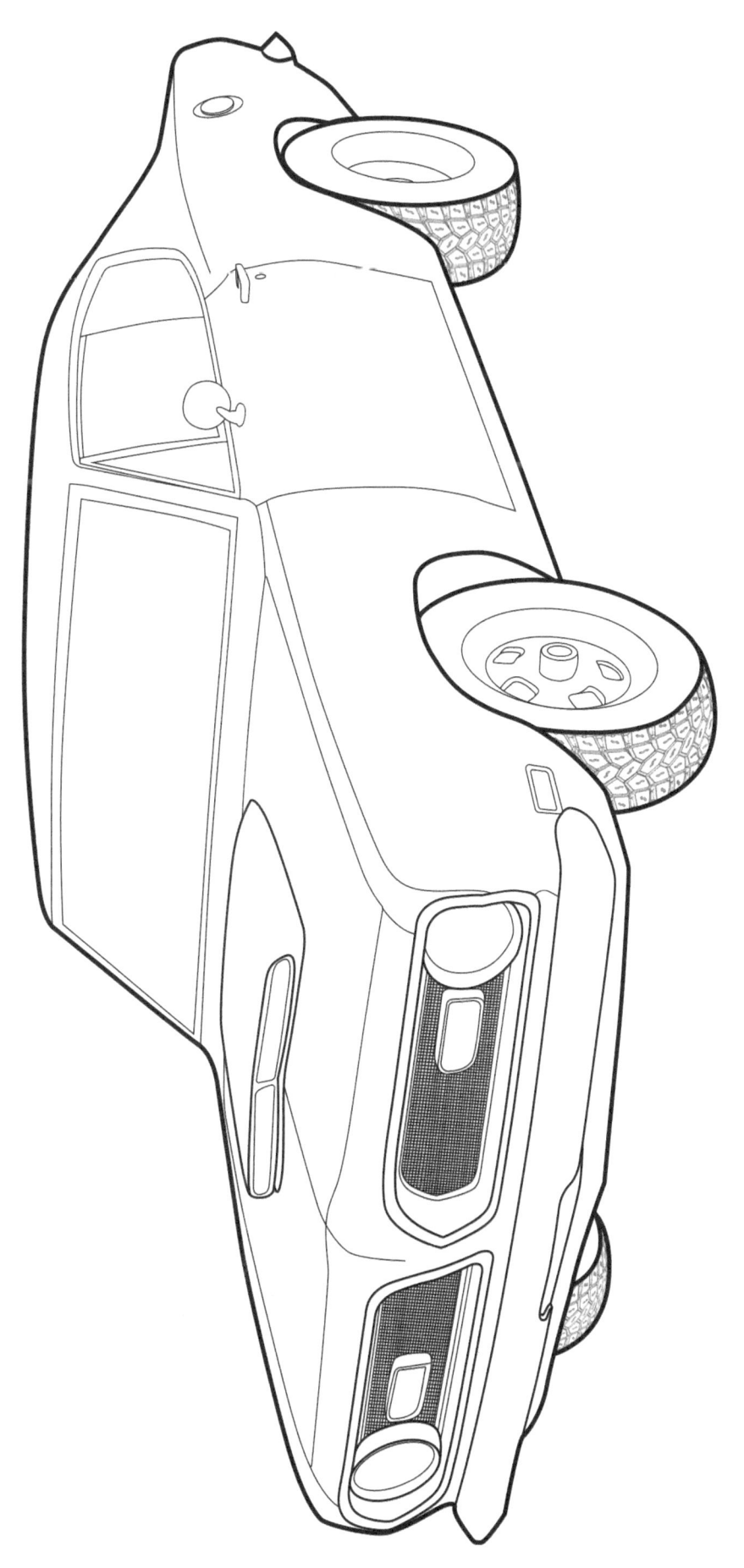

Plymouth Barracuda 1973

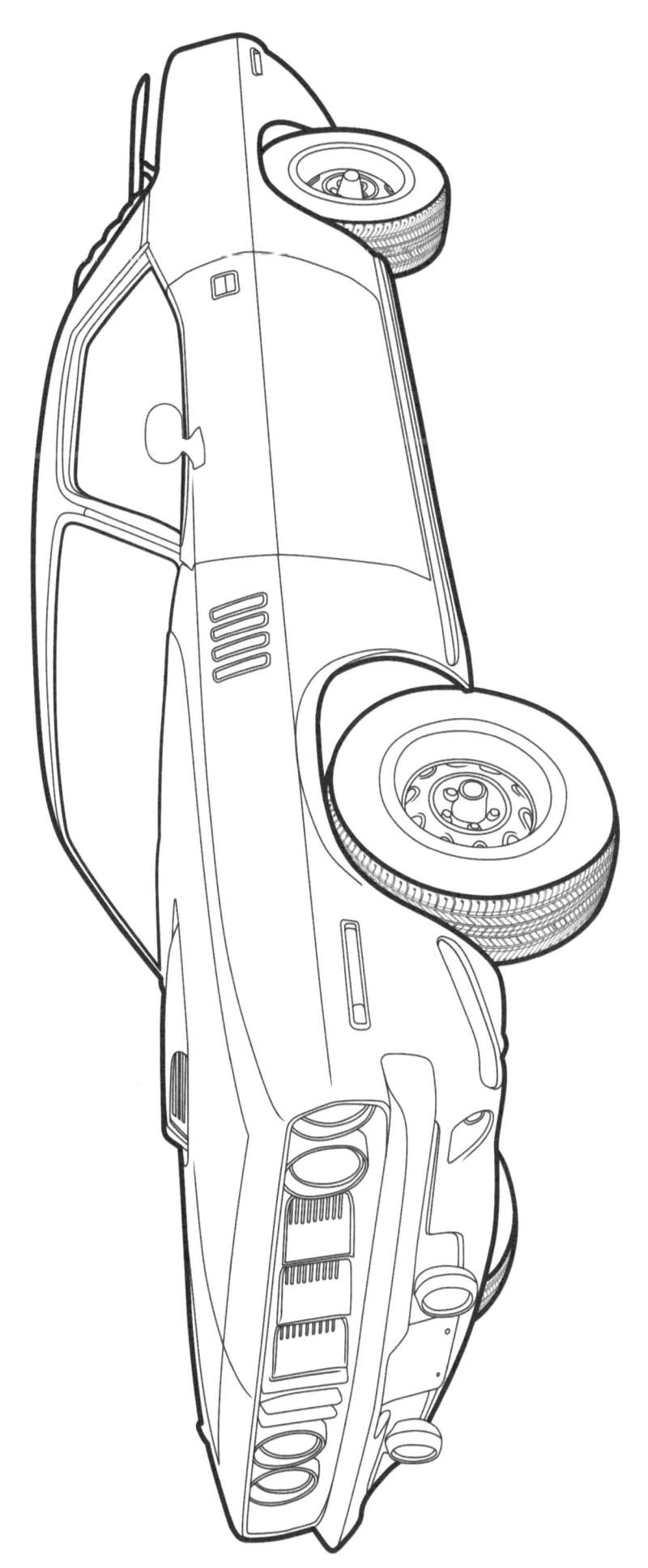

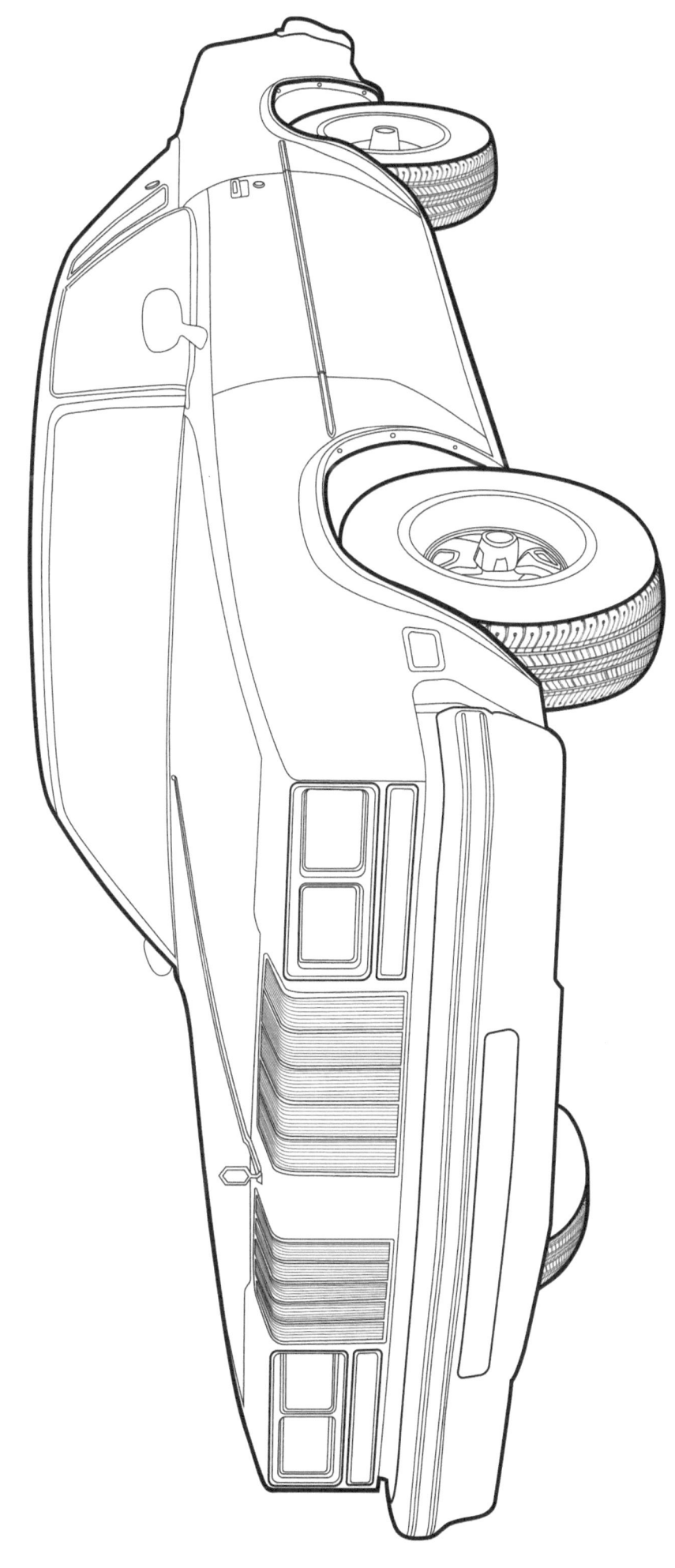

Oldsmobile Rallye 350 1970

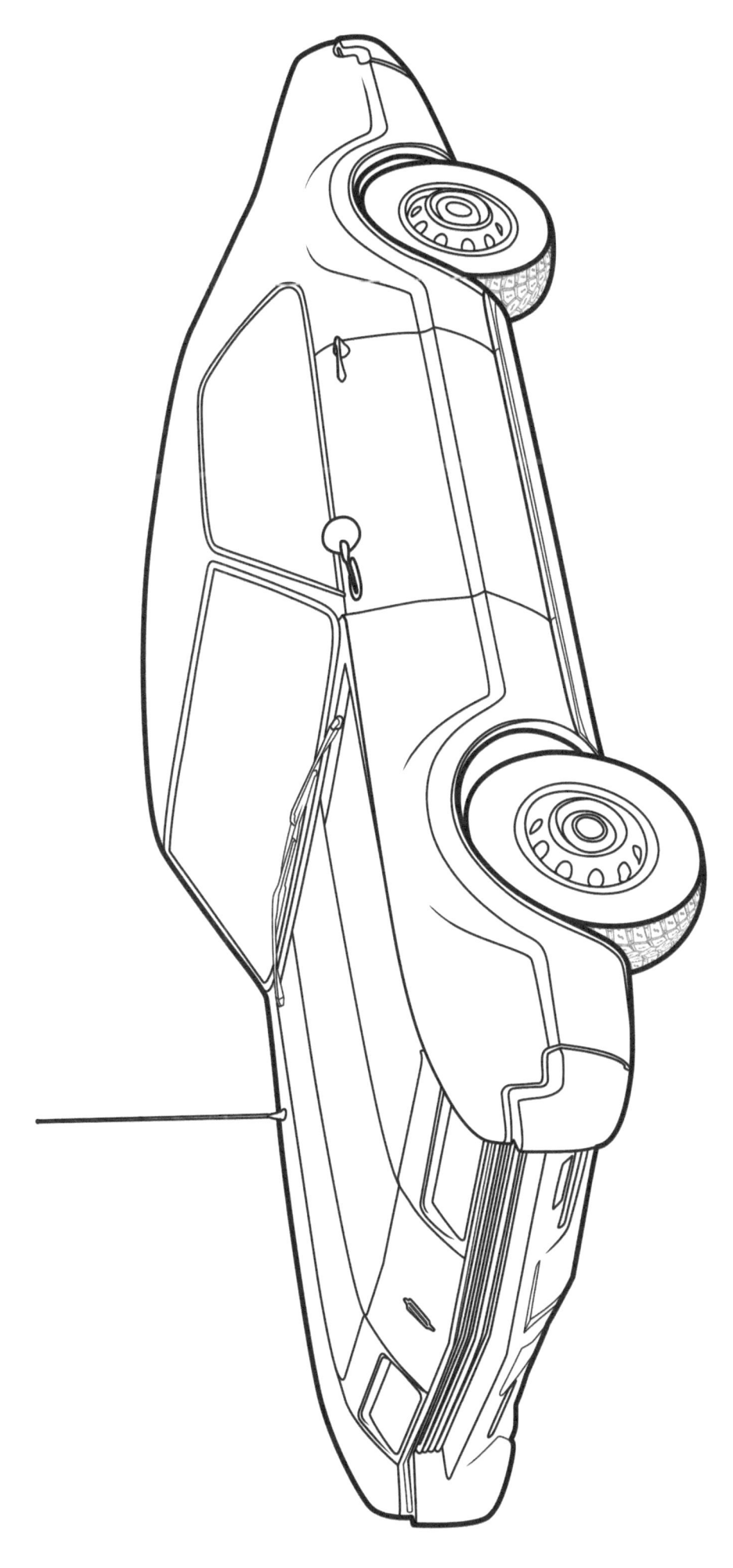

Oldsmobile Toronado 1966

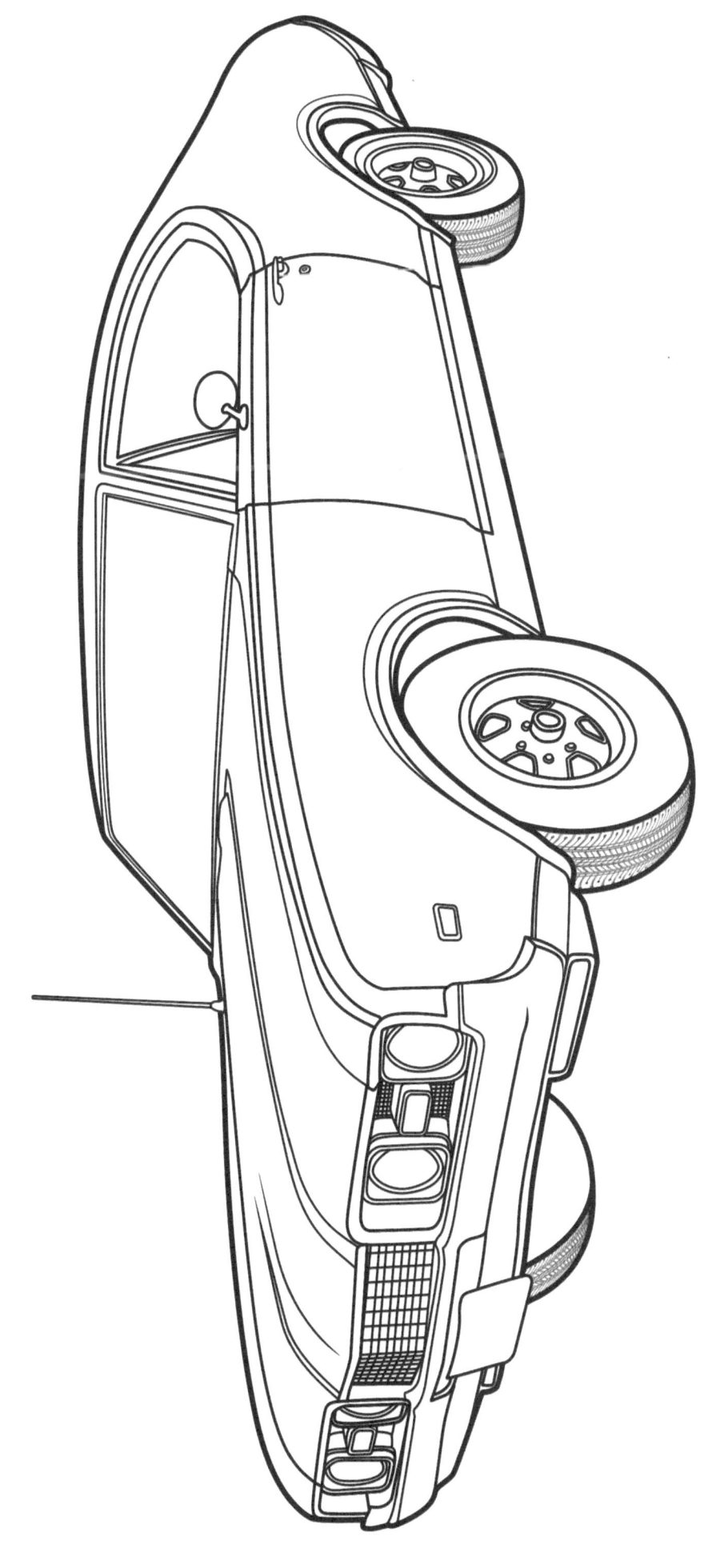

Nissan Skyline 2000 GT-R 1973

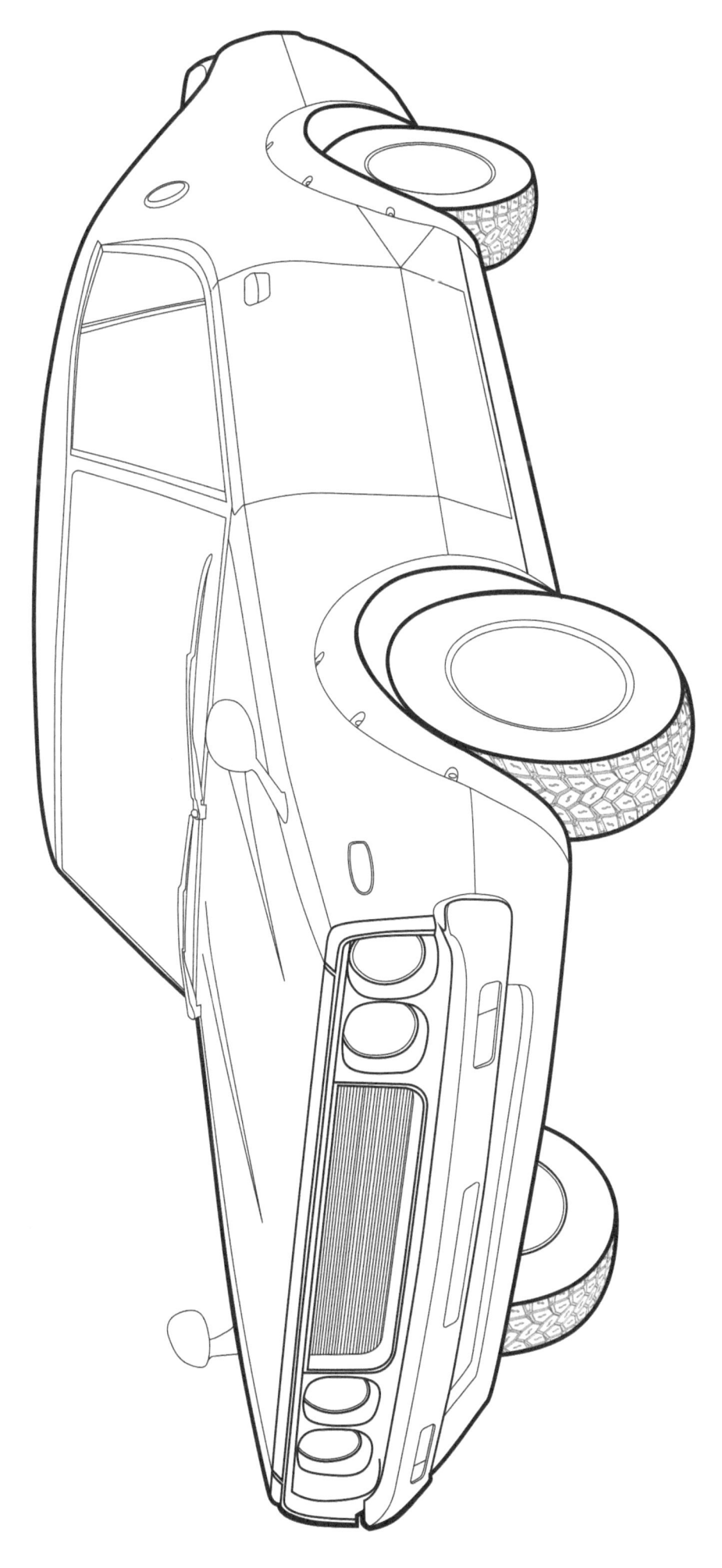

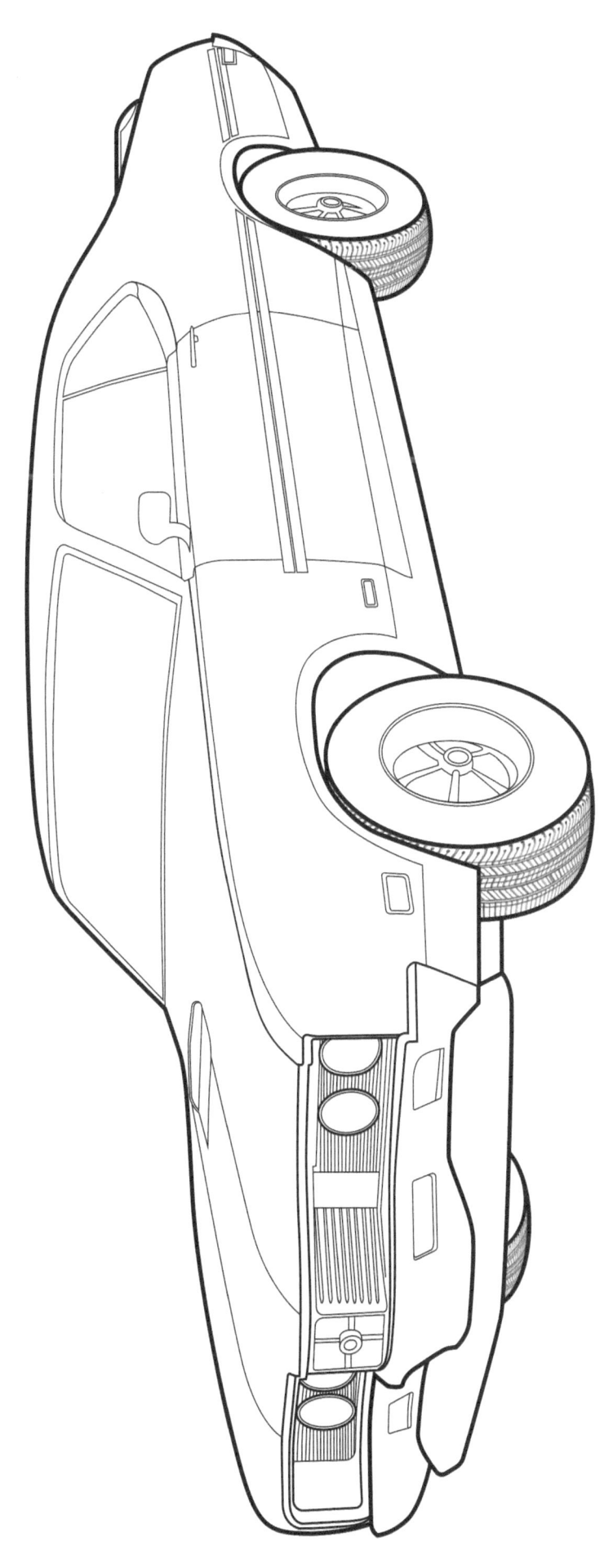

Mercury Cougar Eliminator Boss 429 1967

Ford Torino 1970

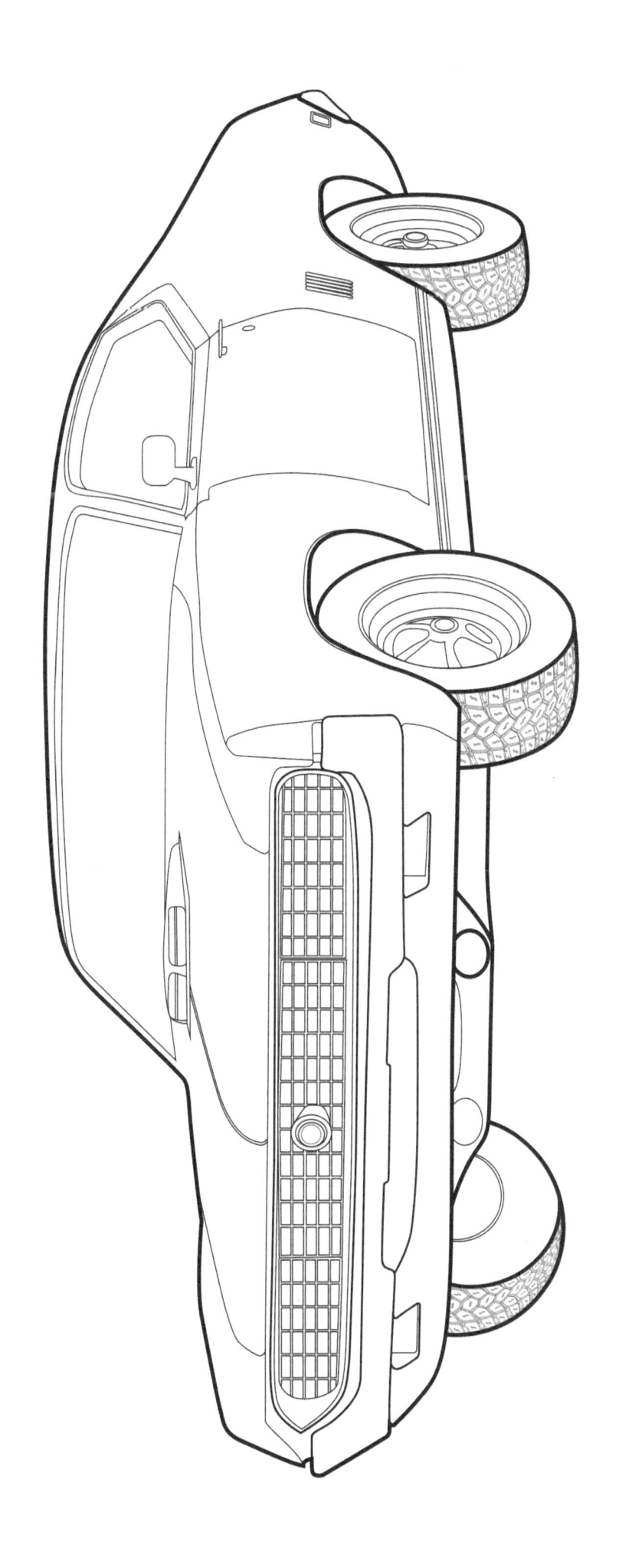

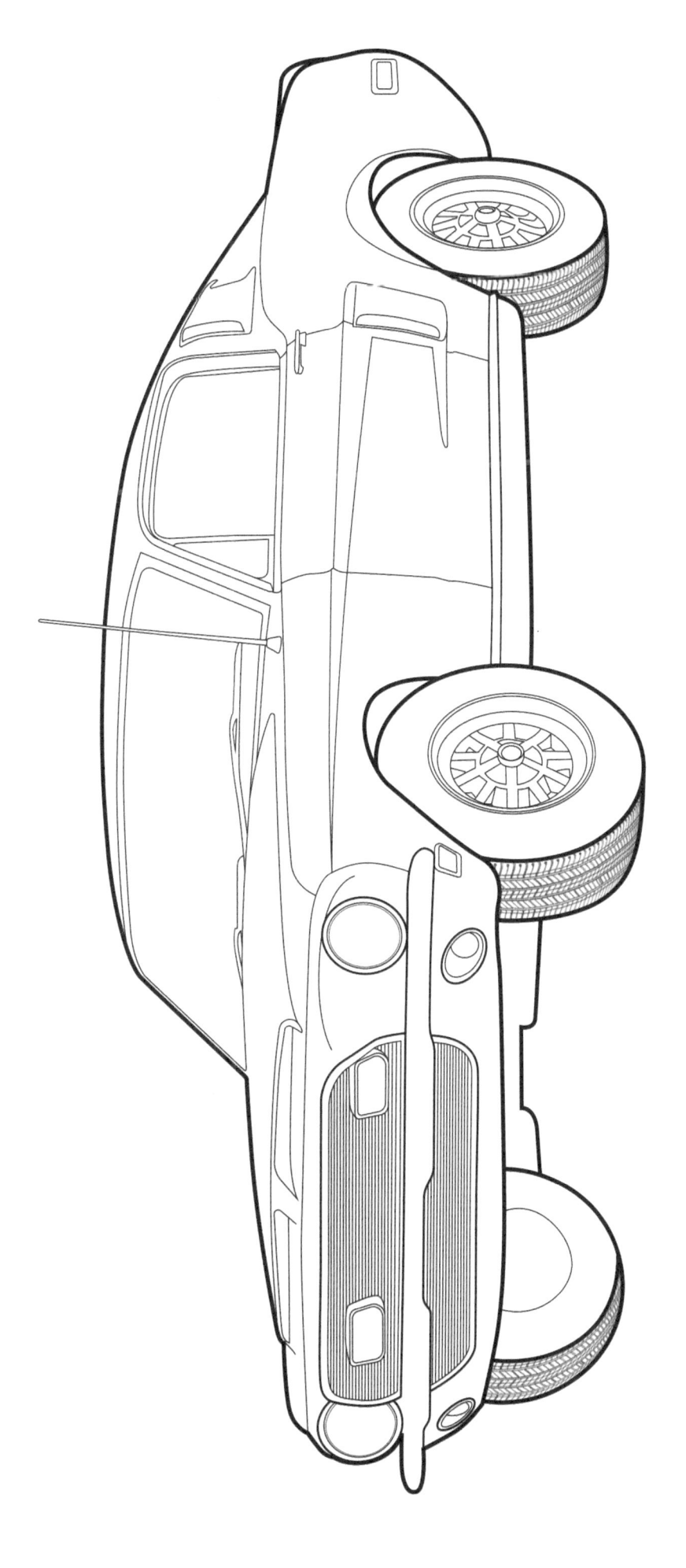

Ford Mustang Shelby 1976

Ford Mustang Boss 429 1969

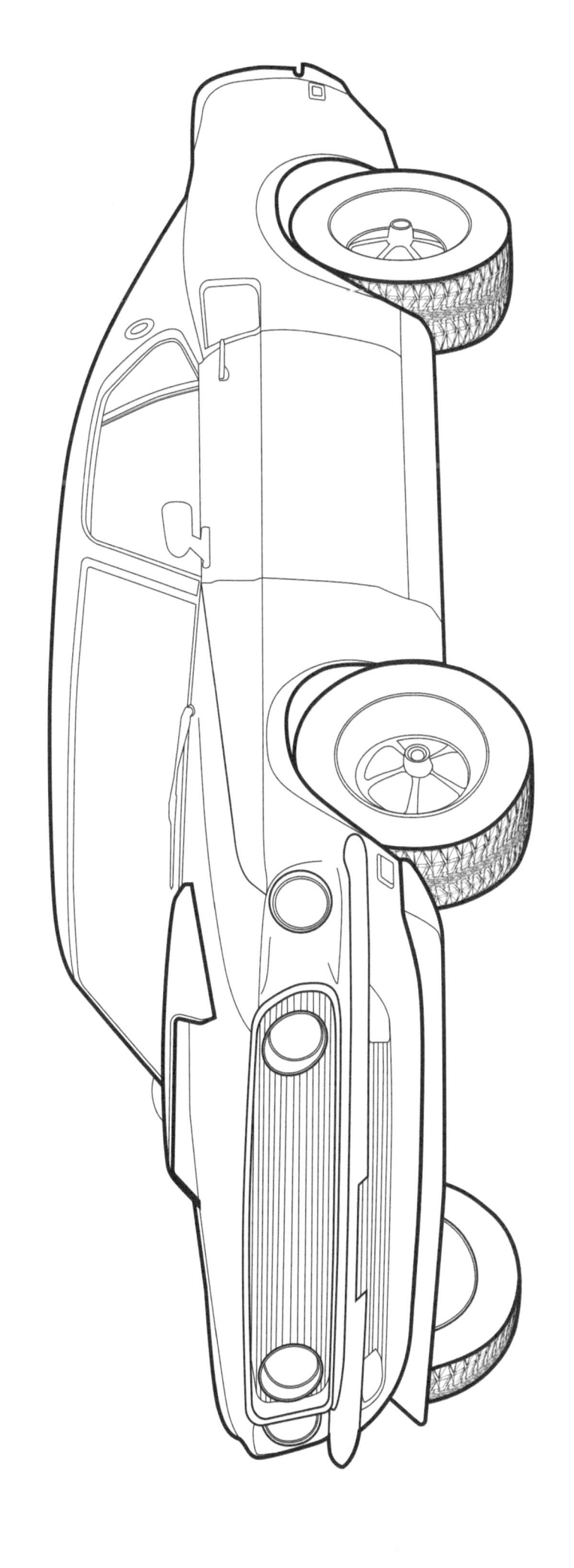

Ford Ranchero 500 1973

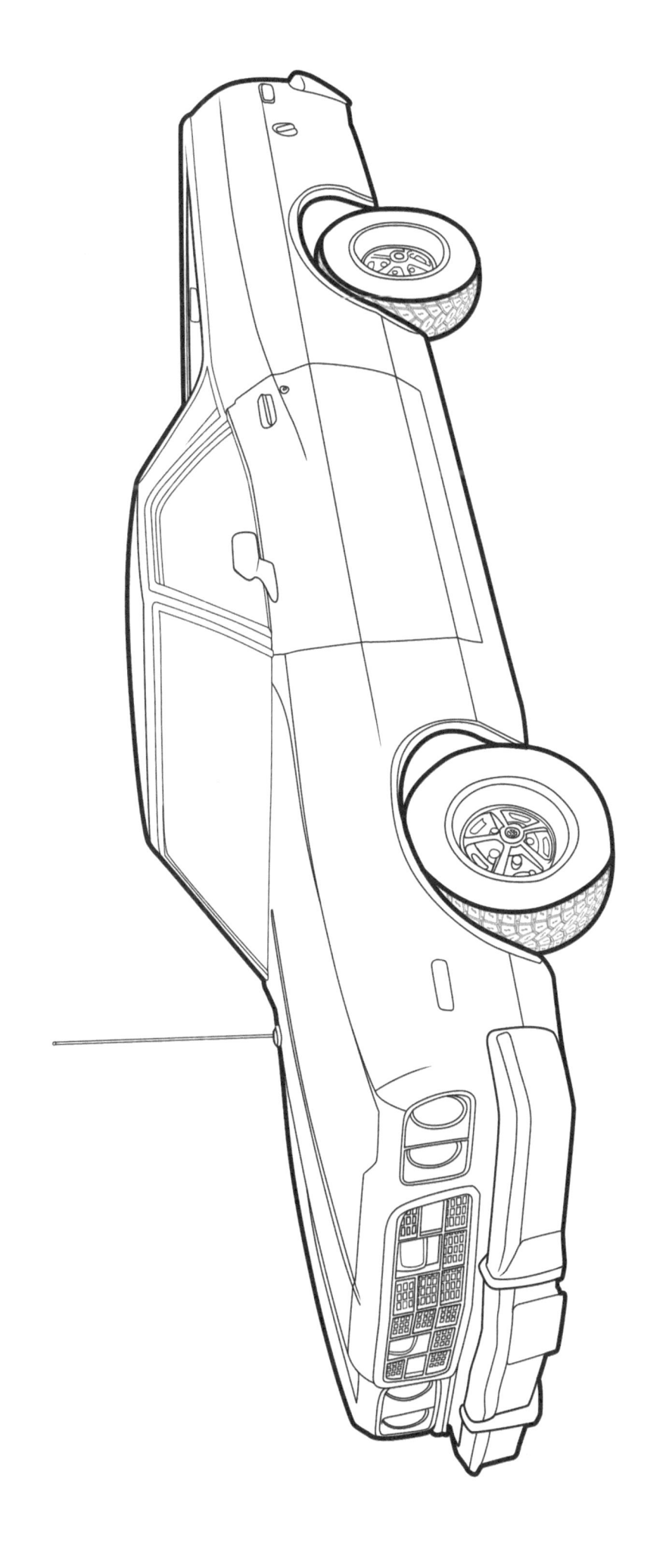

Ford Galaxie Convertible 1959

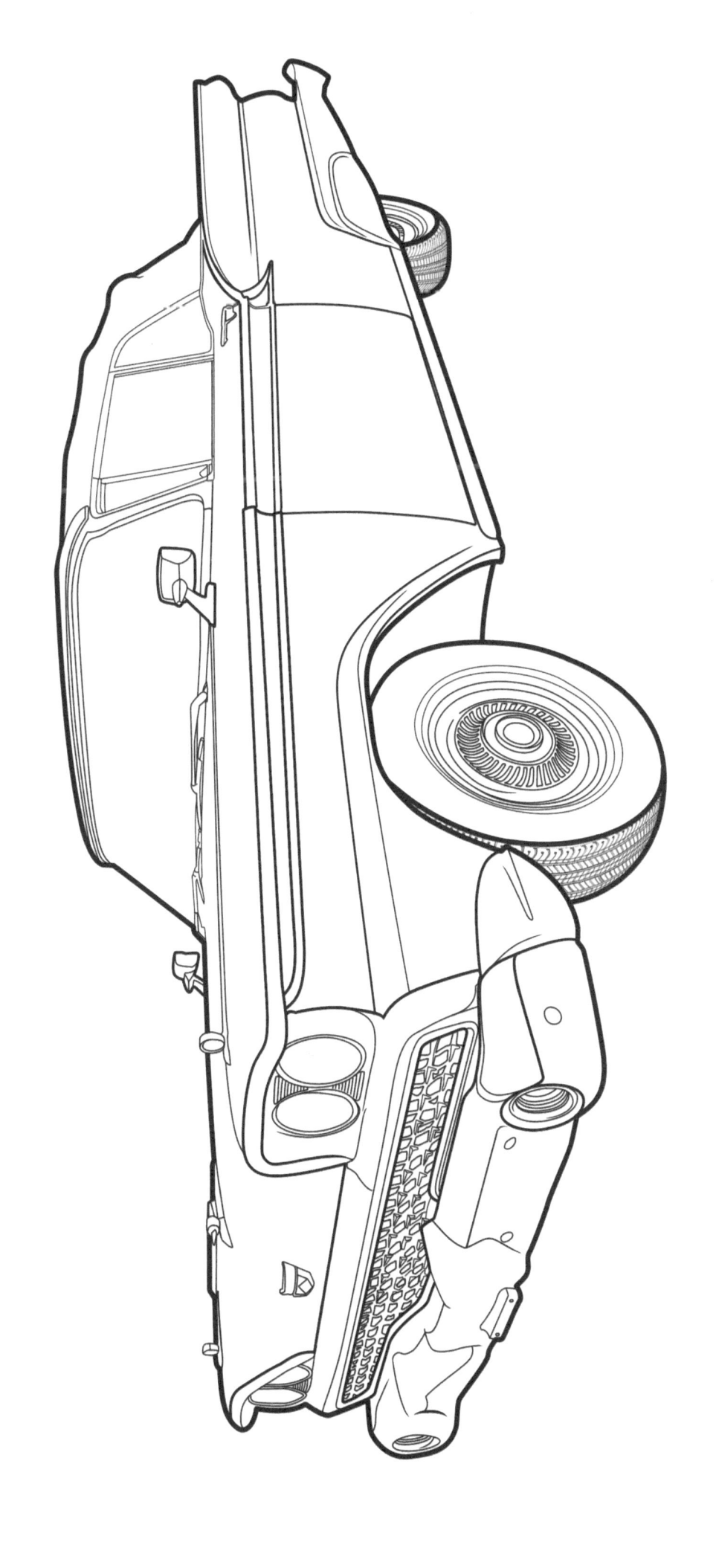

Ford Mustang Dragster 1968

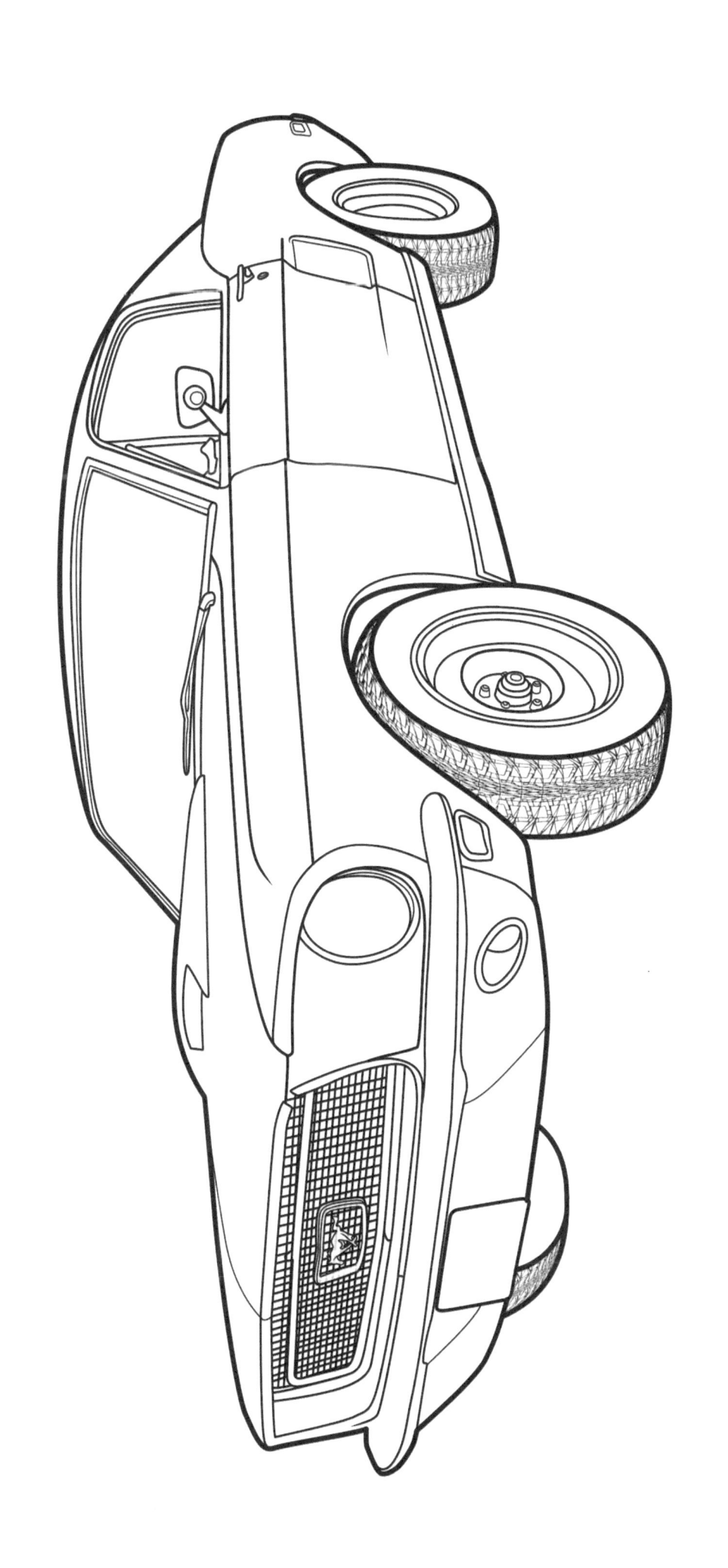

Dodge Viper 1971

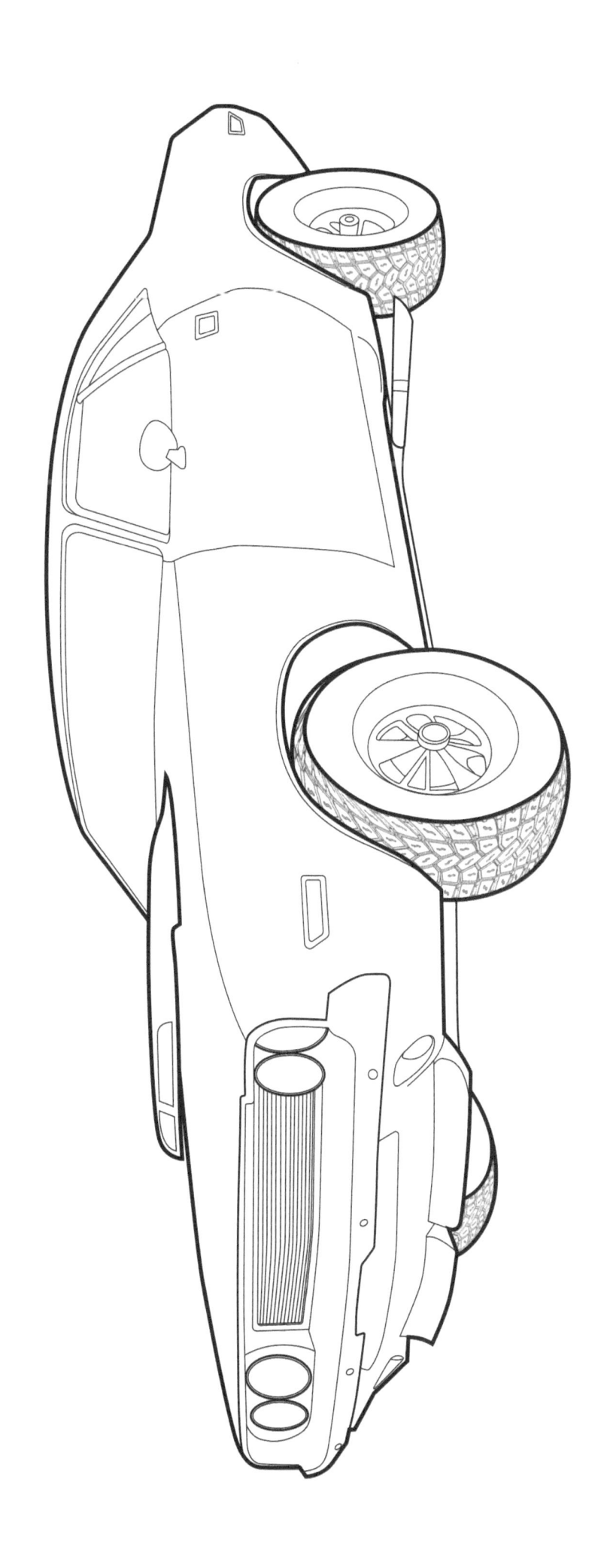

Dodge Coronet 1970

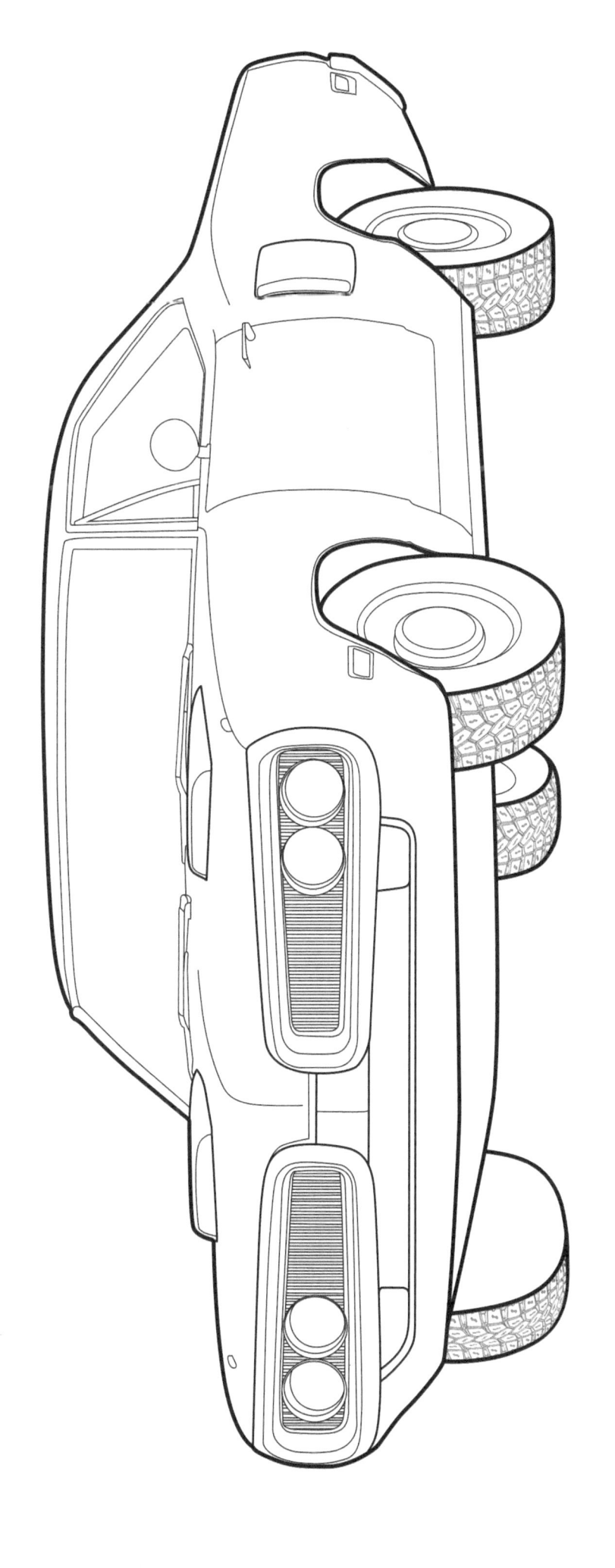

Dodge Charger Daytona 1969

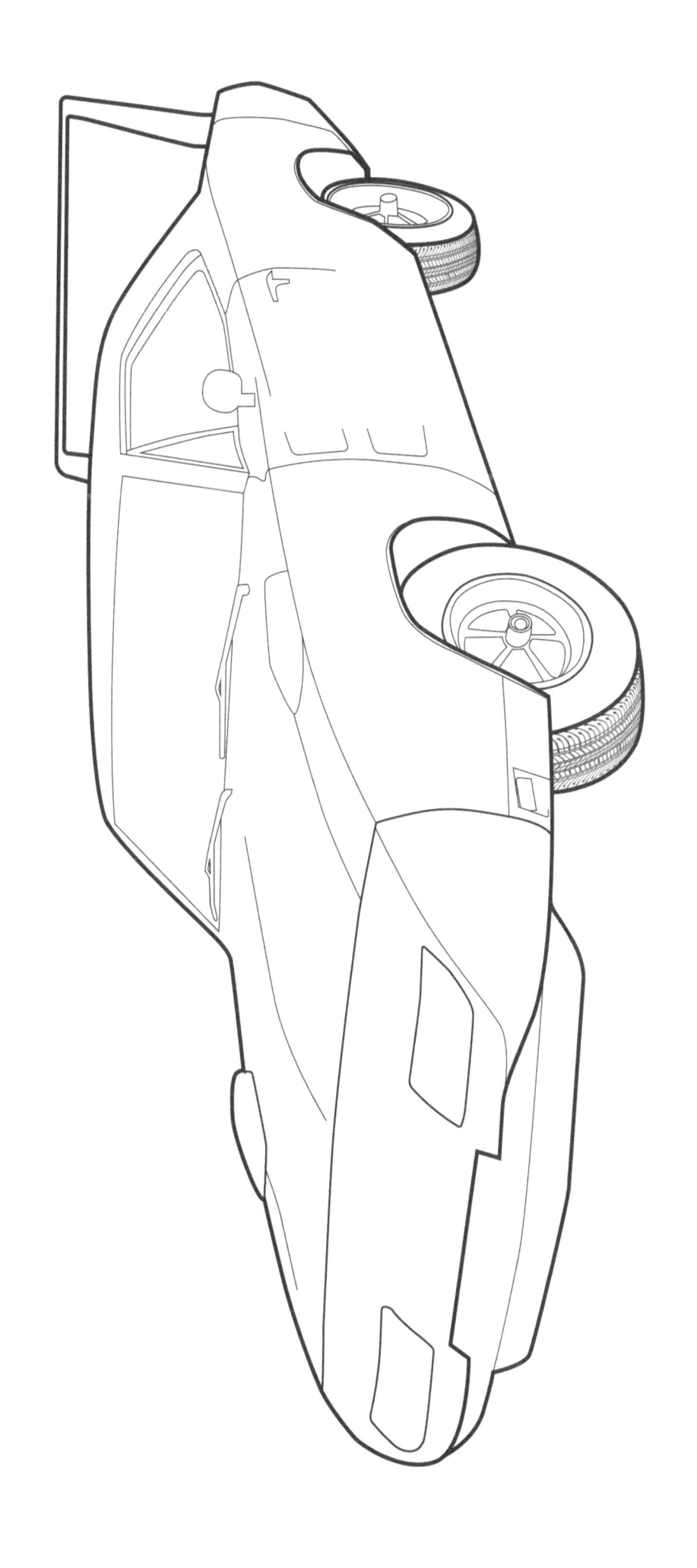

Dodge Challenger 1970

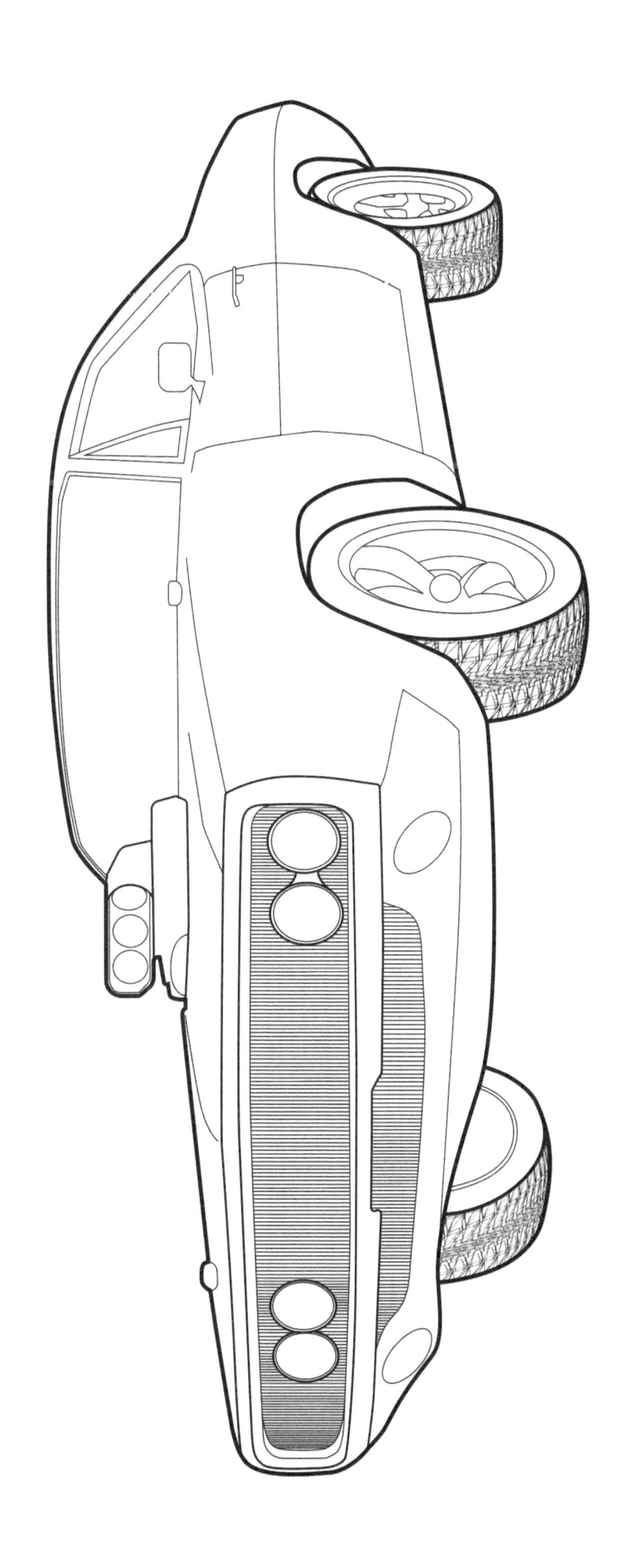

Dodge Charger R/T-SE 1969

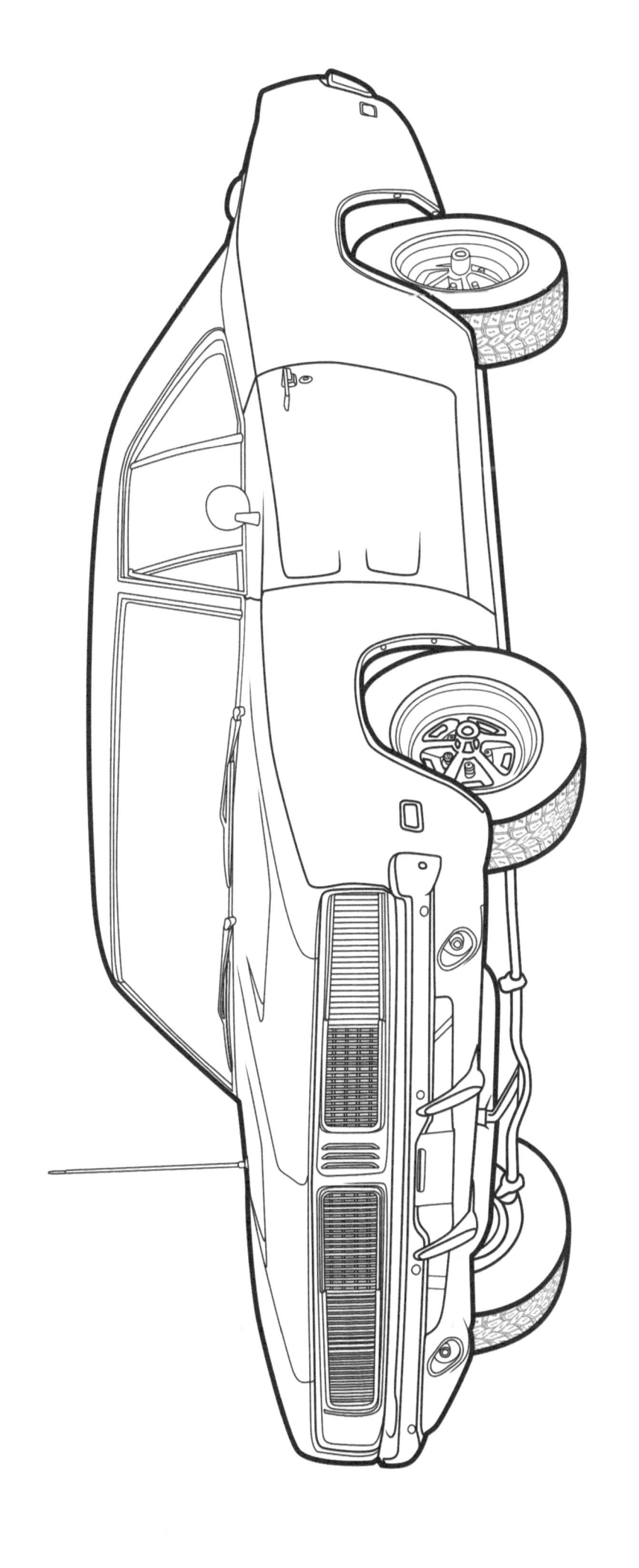

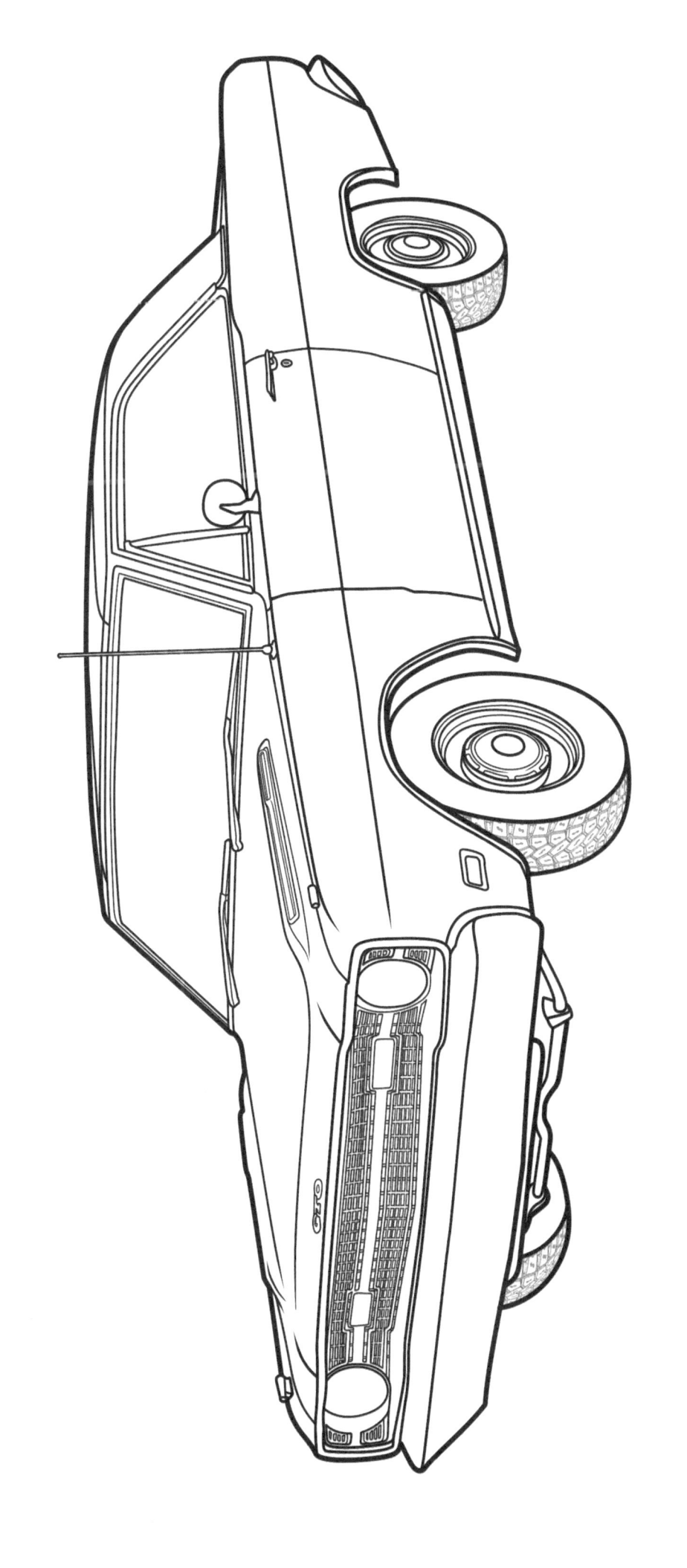

Dodge Dart GTS 440 1969

Chevrolet Nova 1970

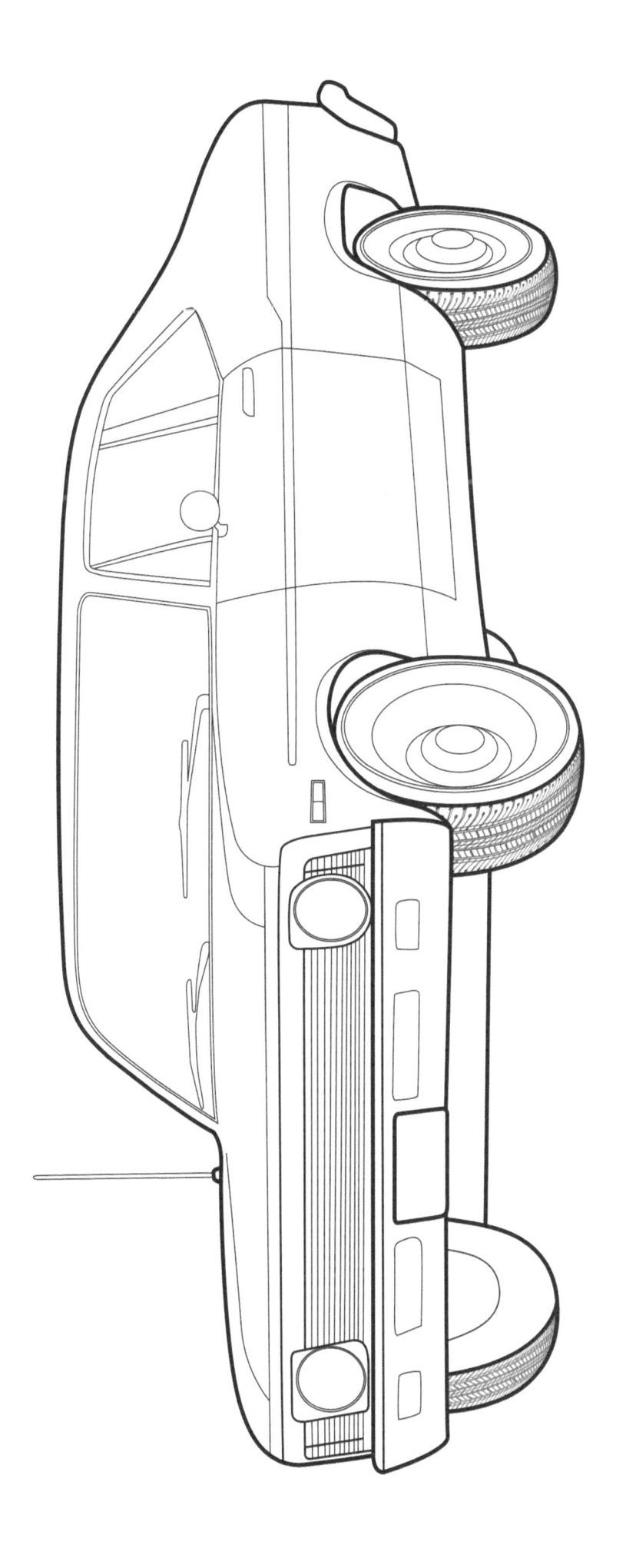

Chevrolet Monte Carlo 1969

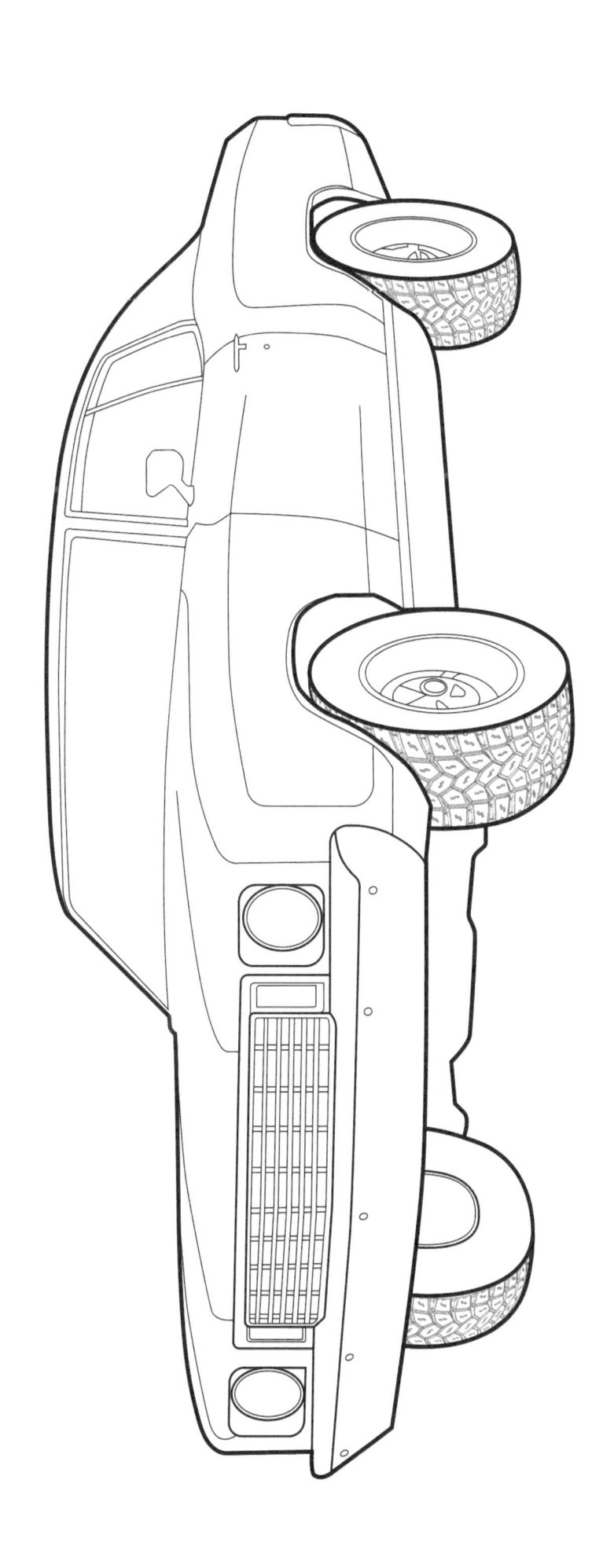

Chevrolet Impala 1967

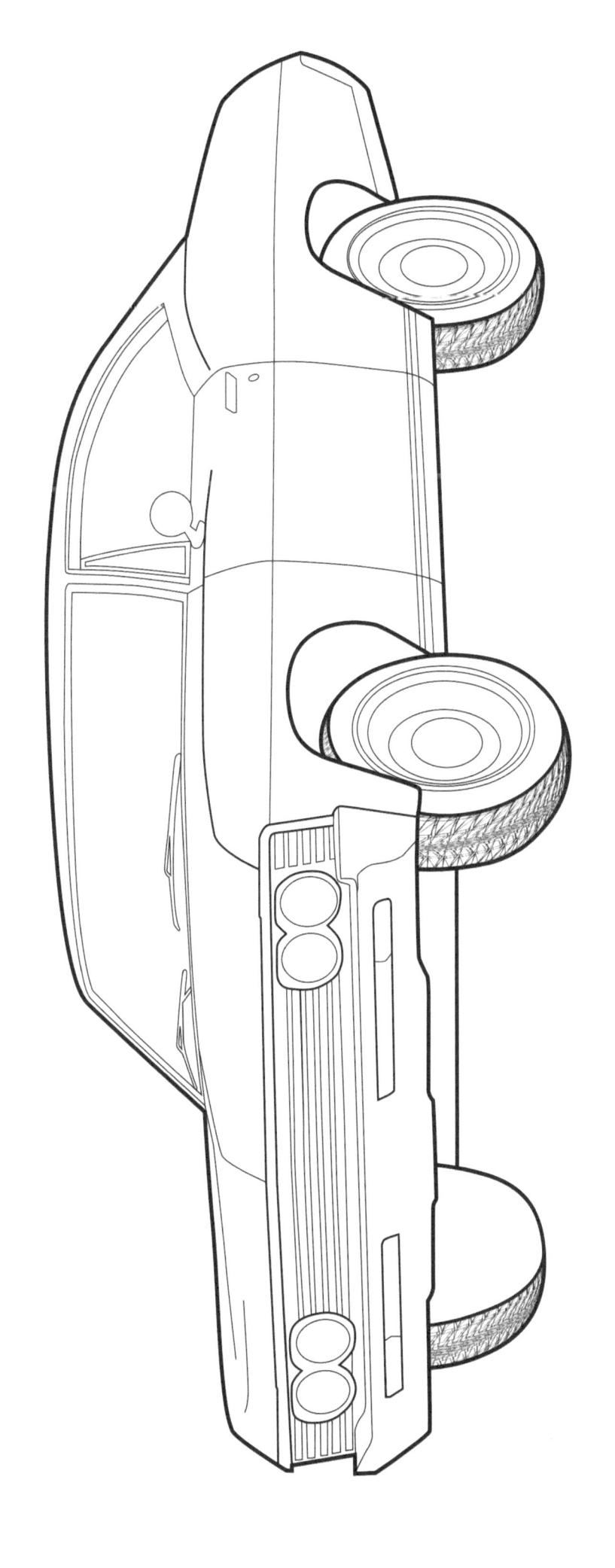

Chevrolet Chevelle 1967

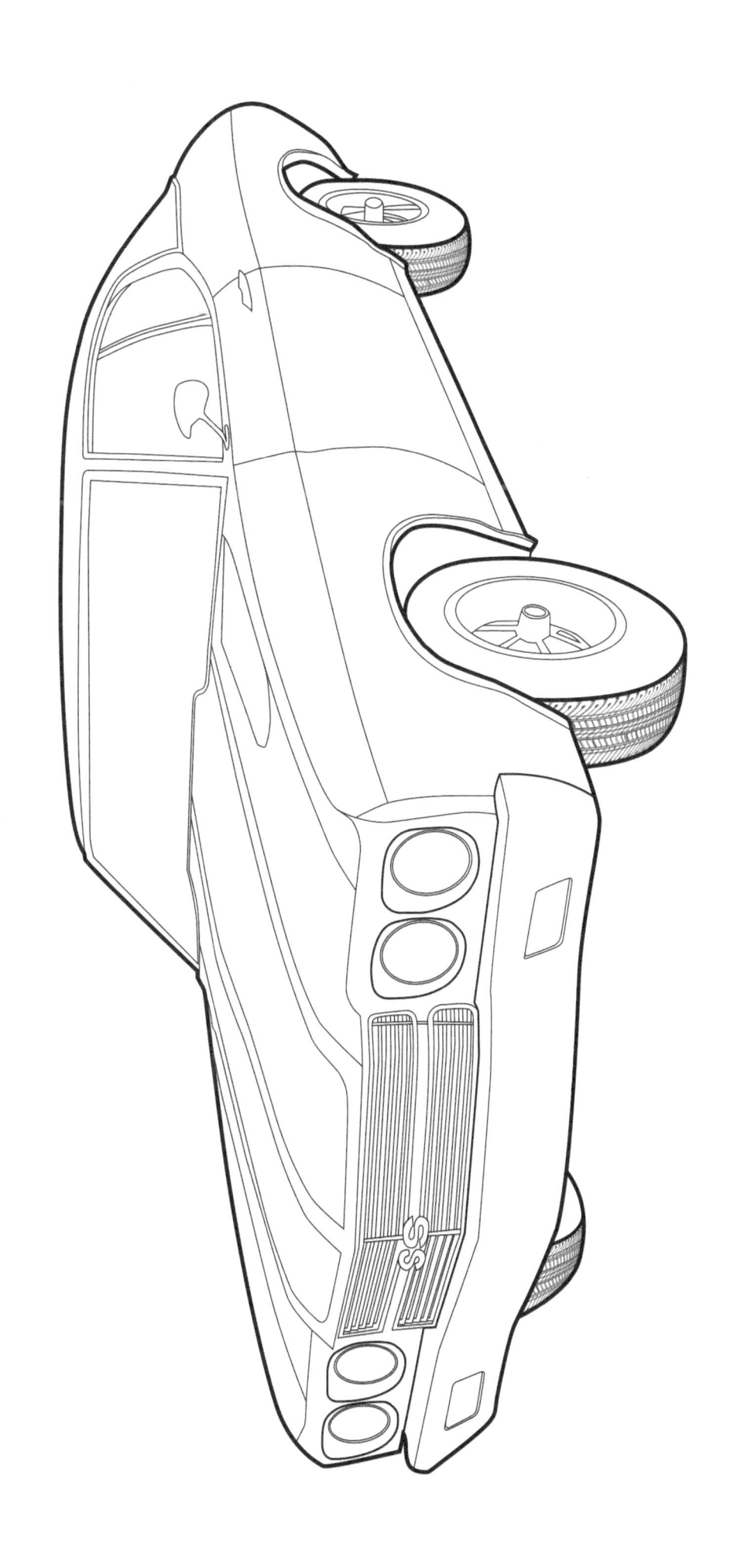

Chevrolet Camaro 1969

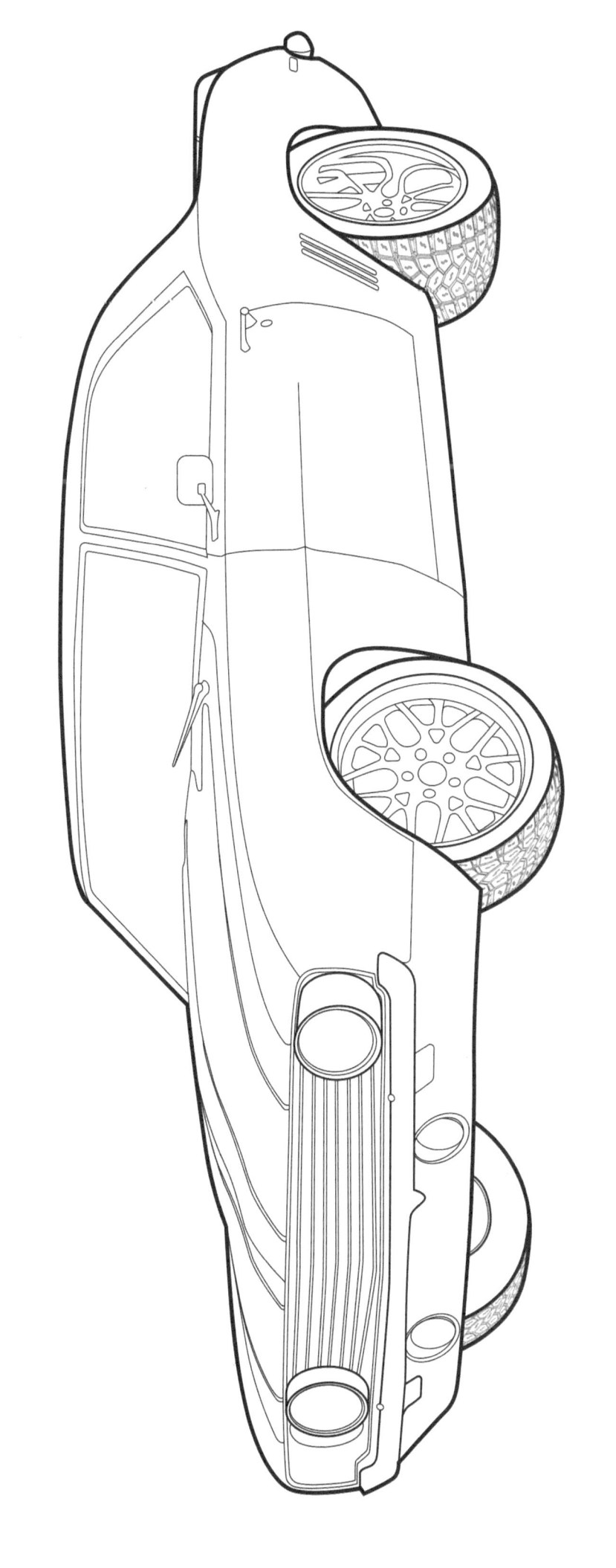

Chevrolet El Camino SS 454 1970

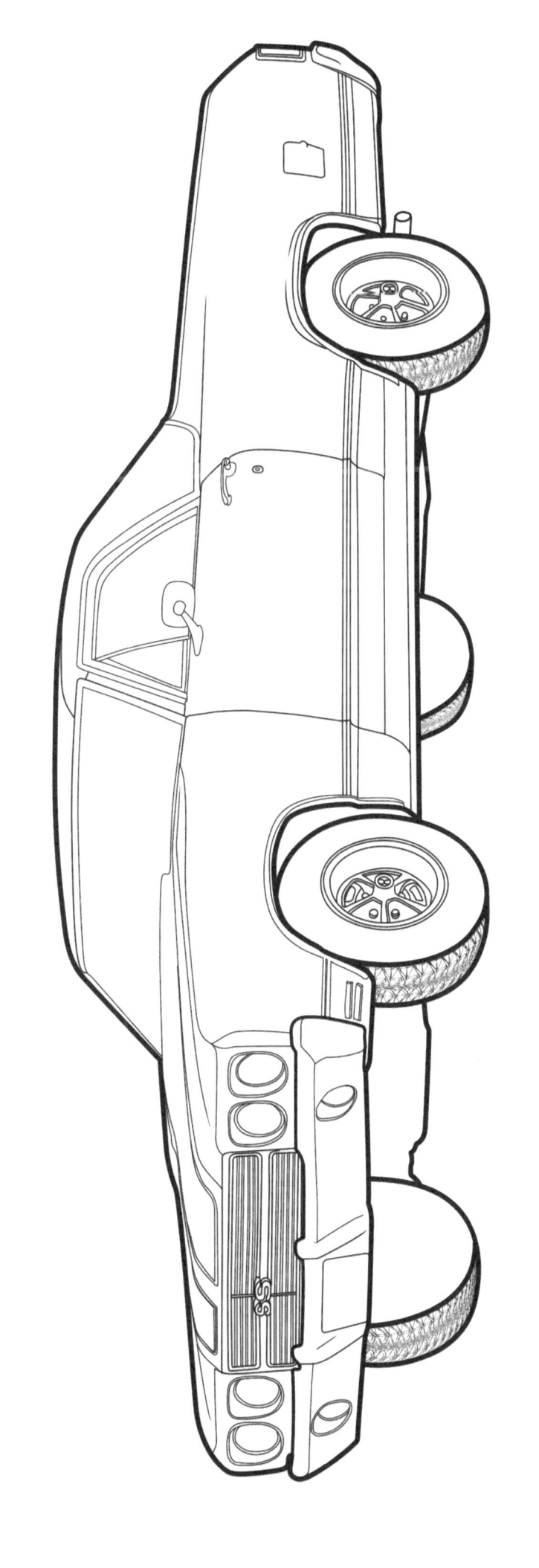

Chevrolet Corvette ZL1 1969

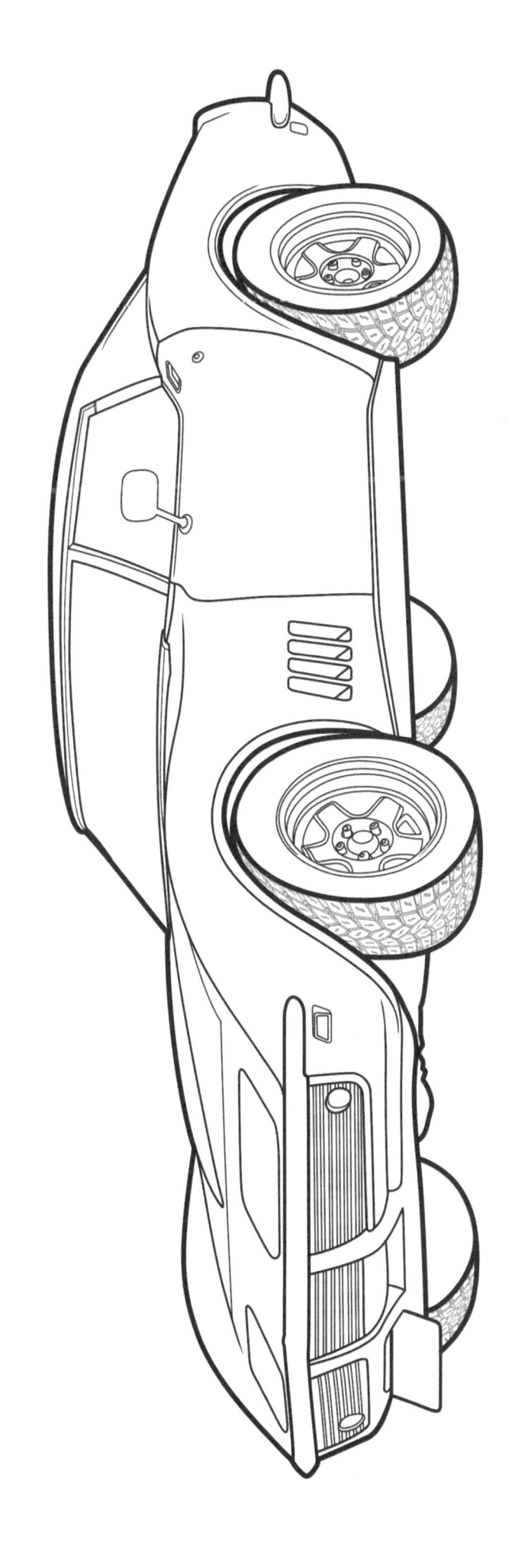

Chevrolet Chevelle Malibu SS 1965

Chevrolet Camaro Yenko RS/SS 427 1968

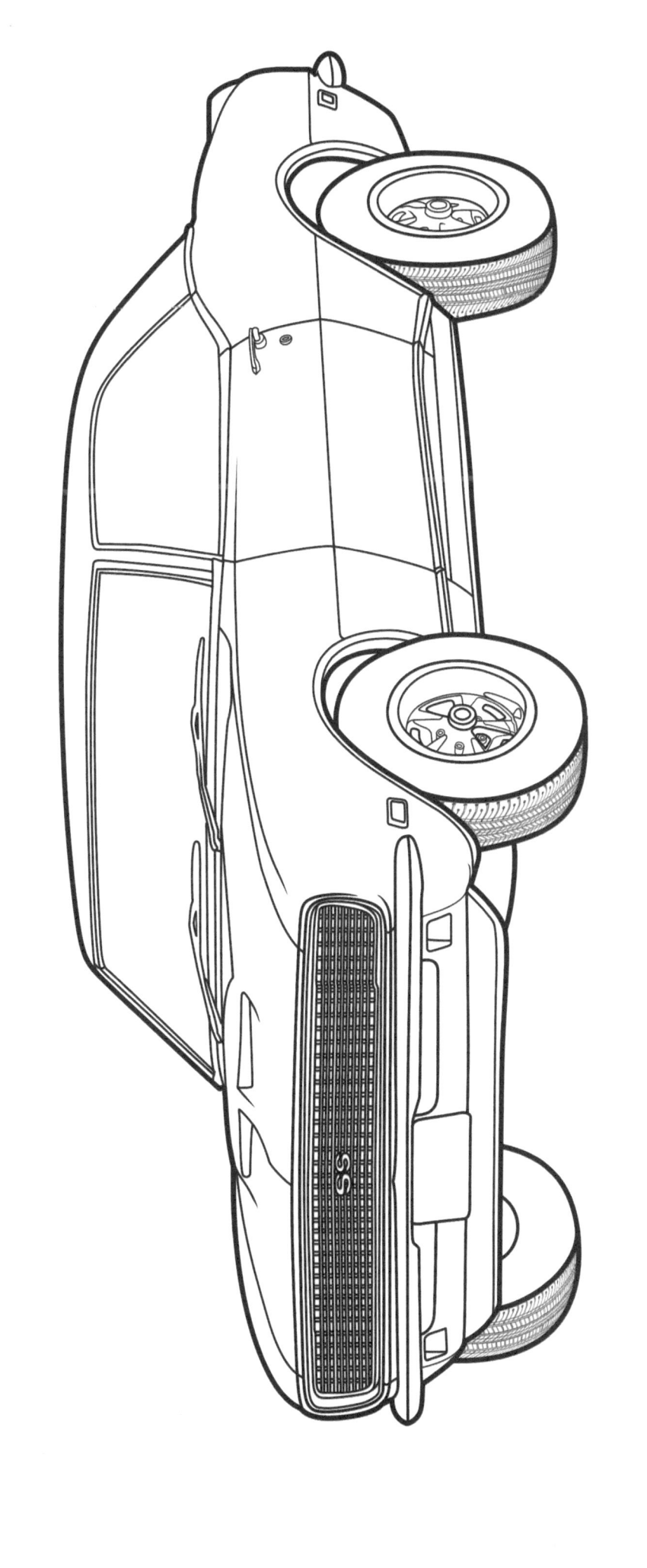

Chevrolet Camaro Z/28 1968

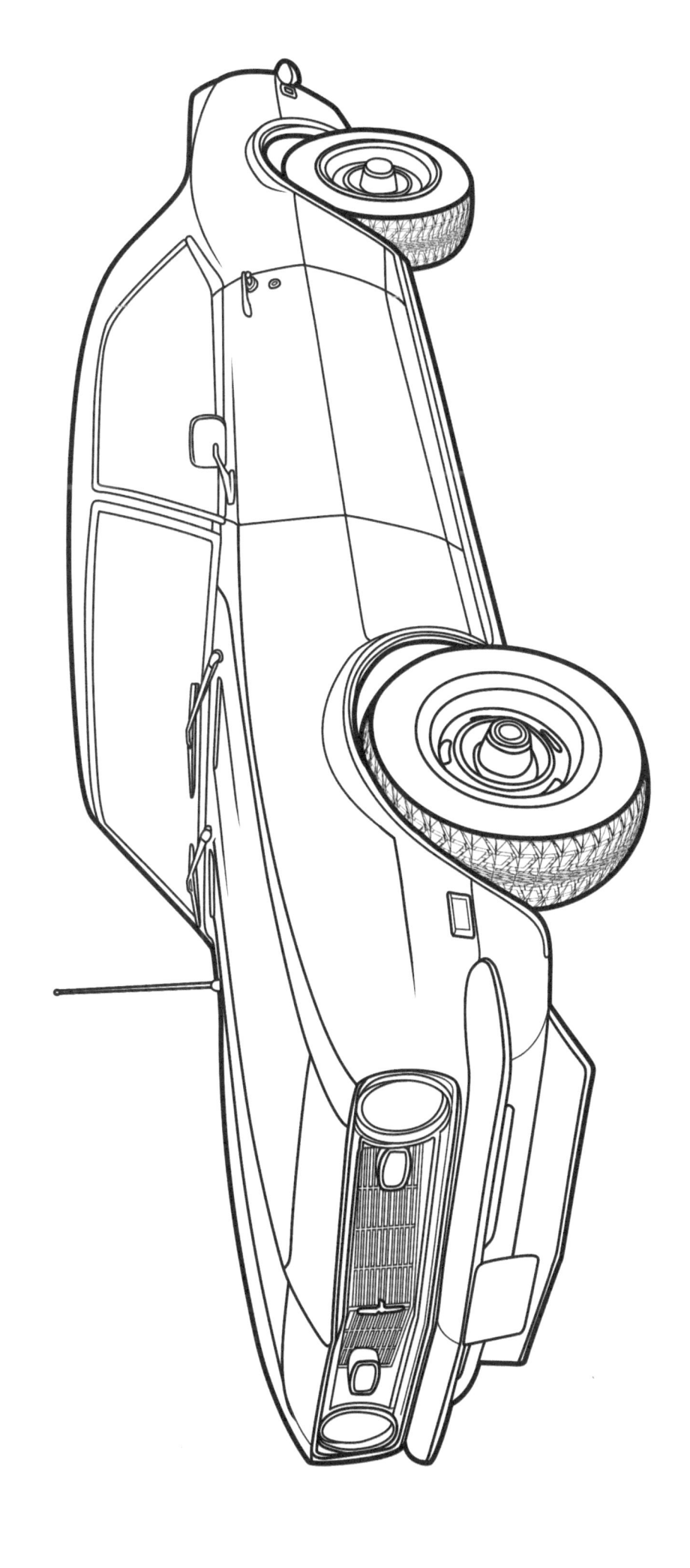

Buick Skylark 1967

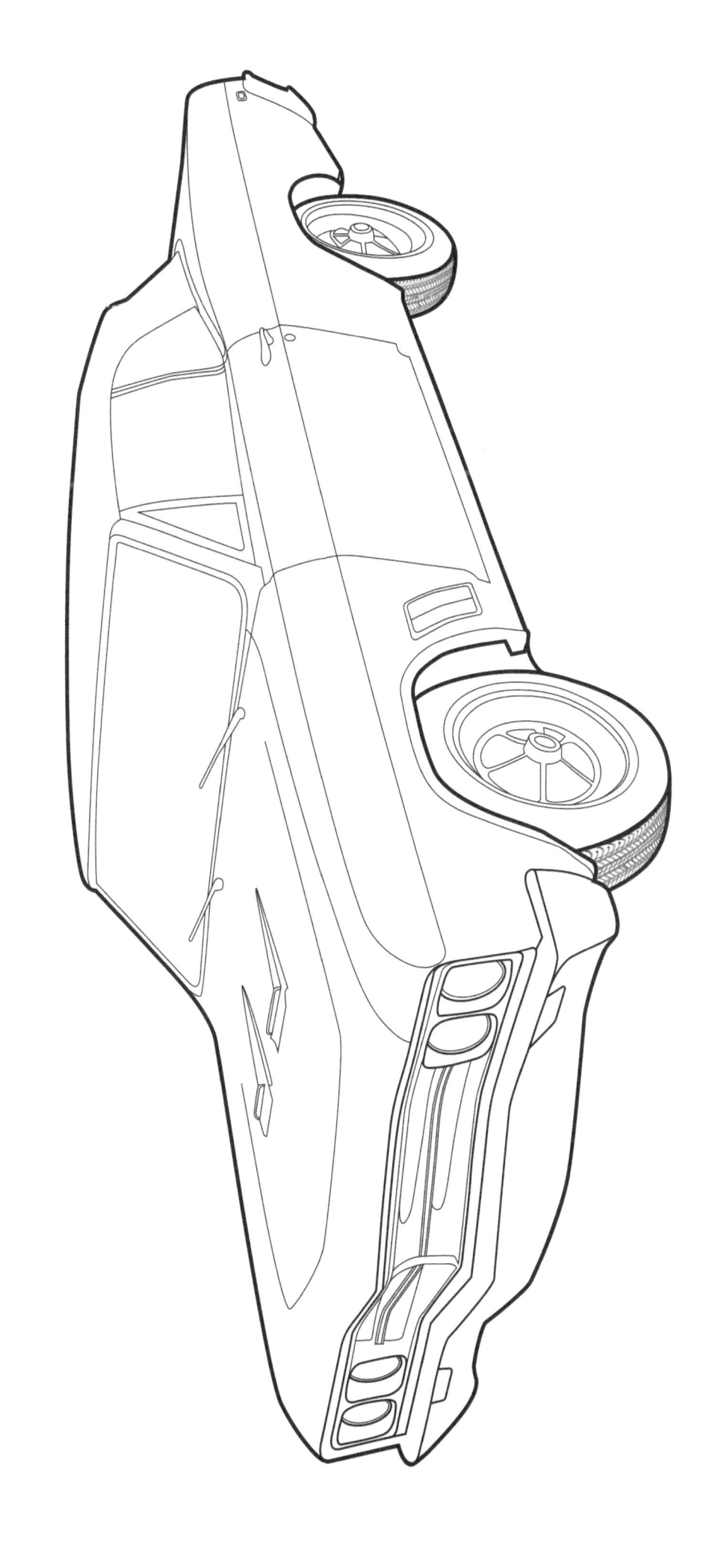

Buick Gran Sport 1965

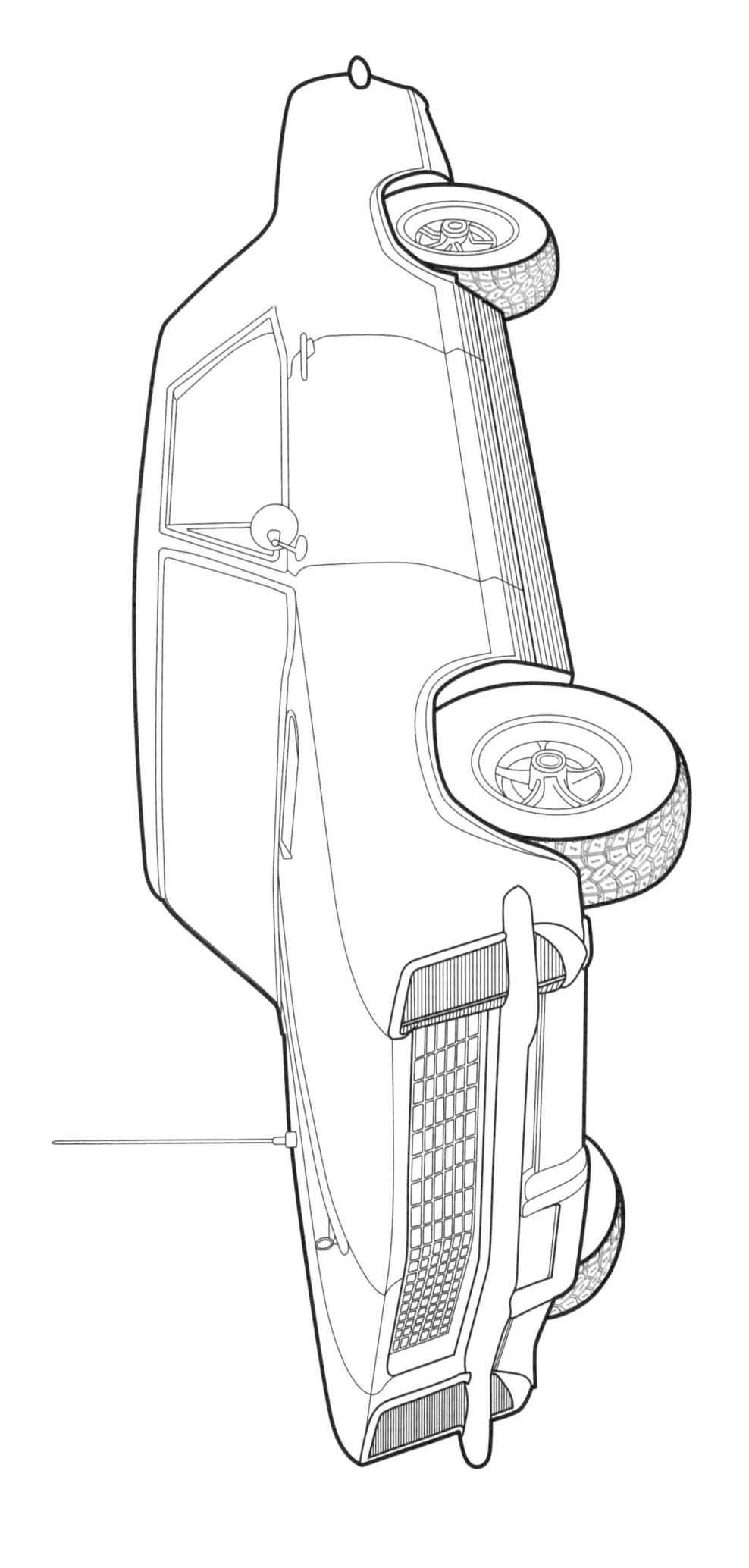

AMC Javelin 1970

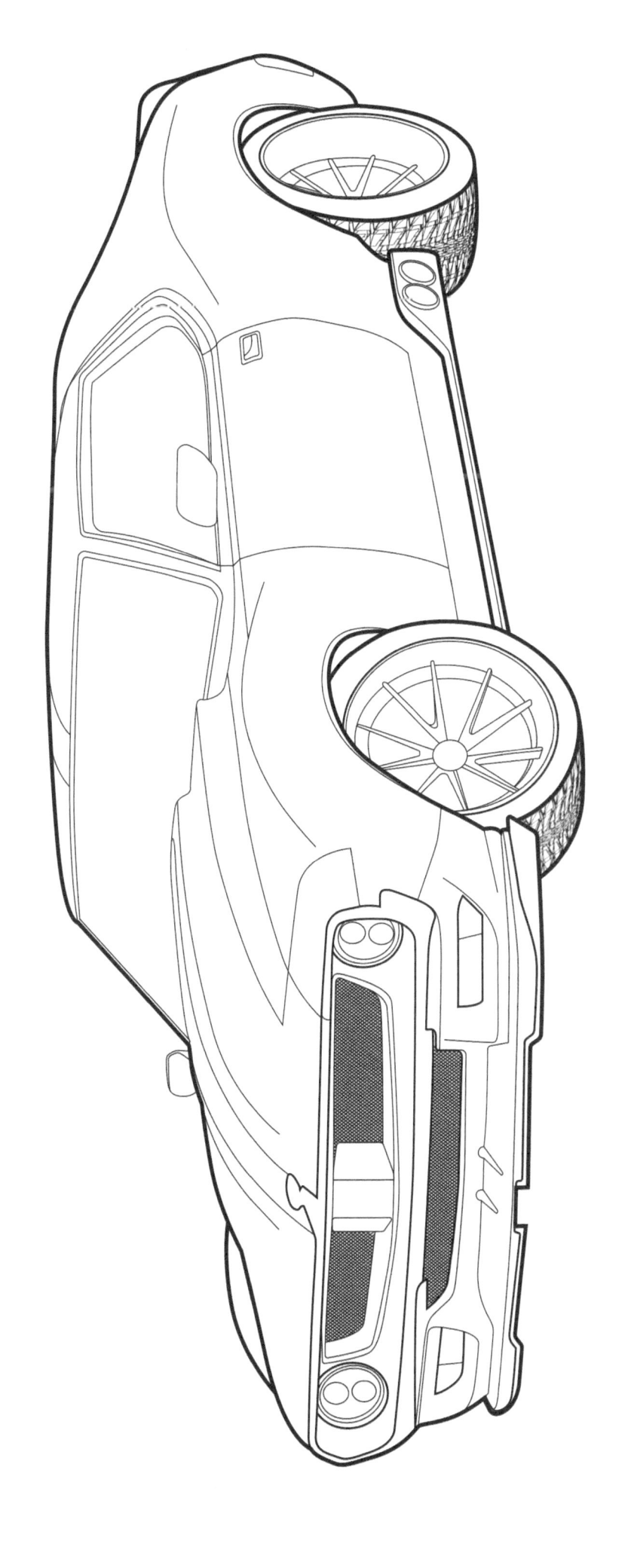

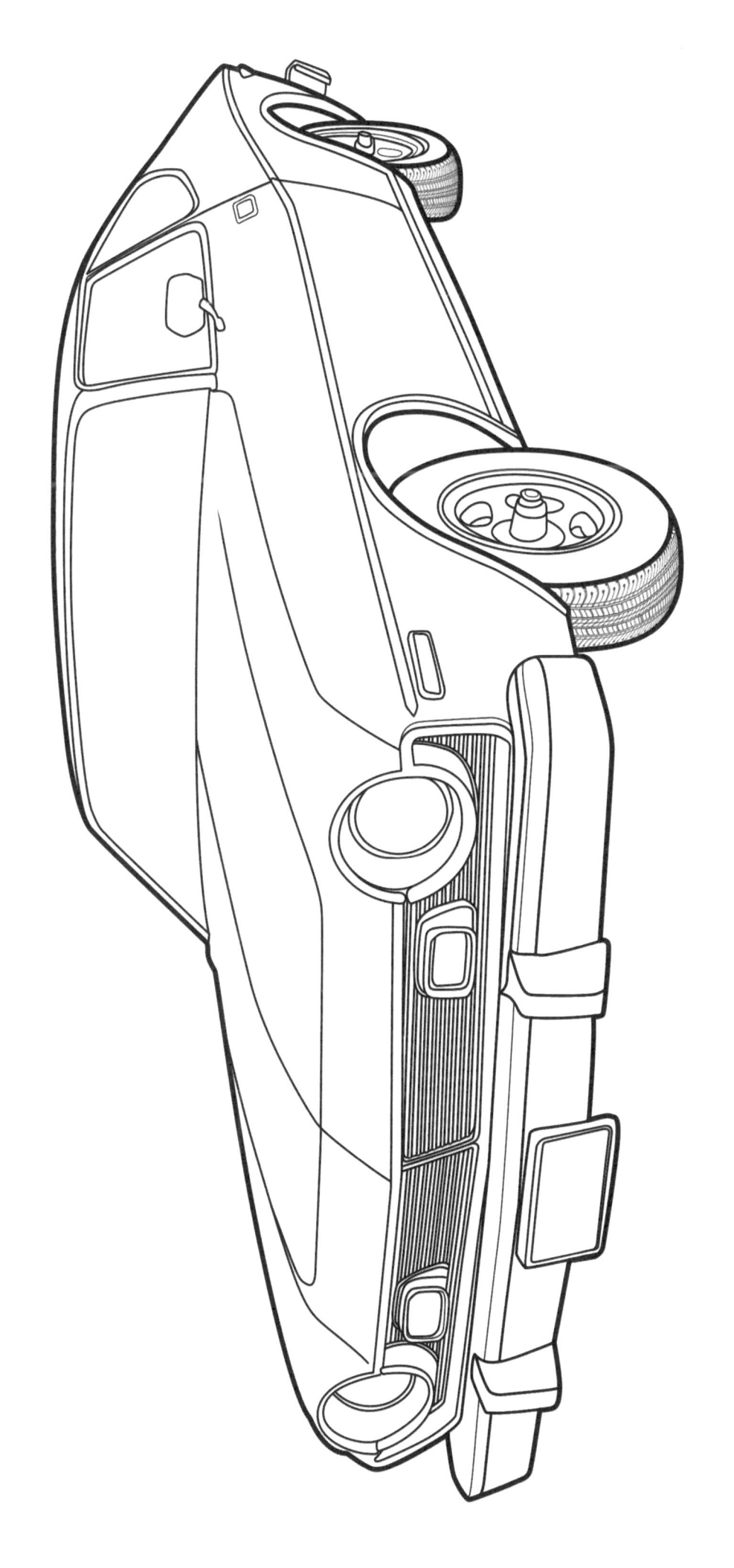

AMC Matador "Machine" 1971

AMC Rebel The Machine 1970

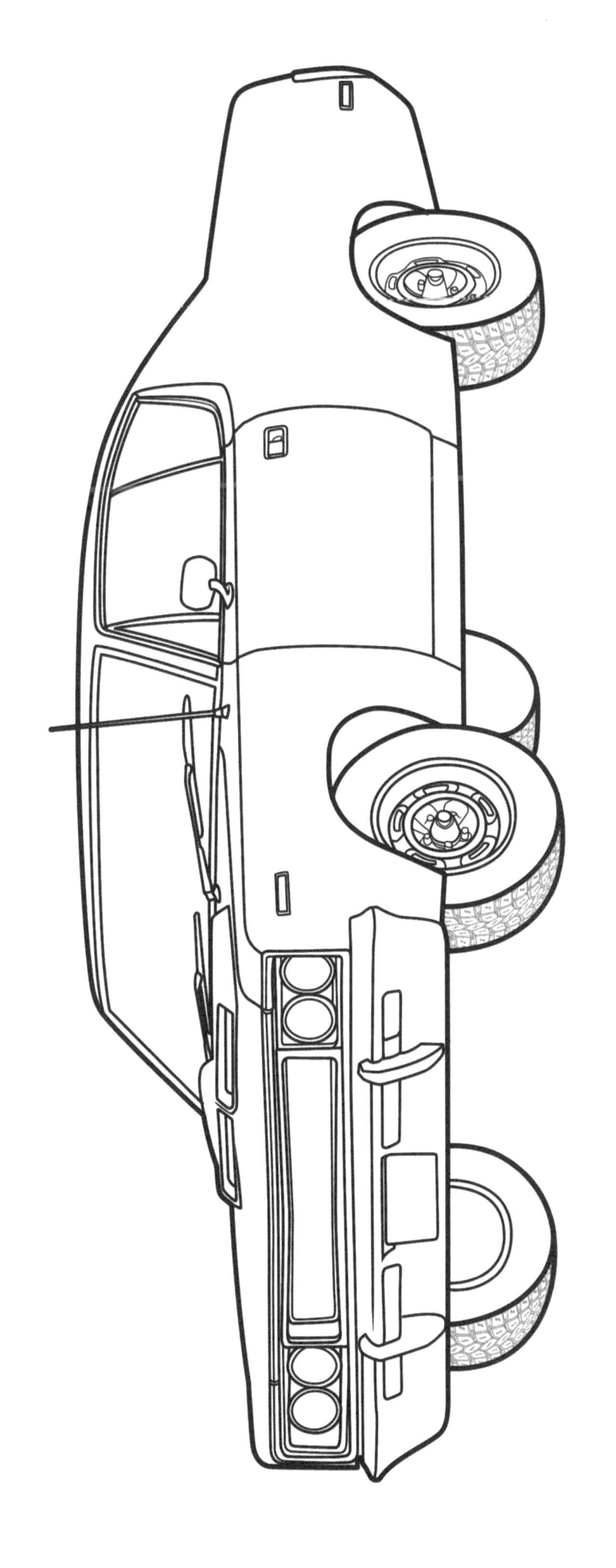

AMC Hornet SC/360 1971

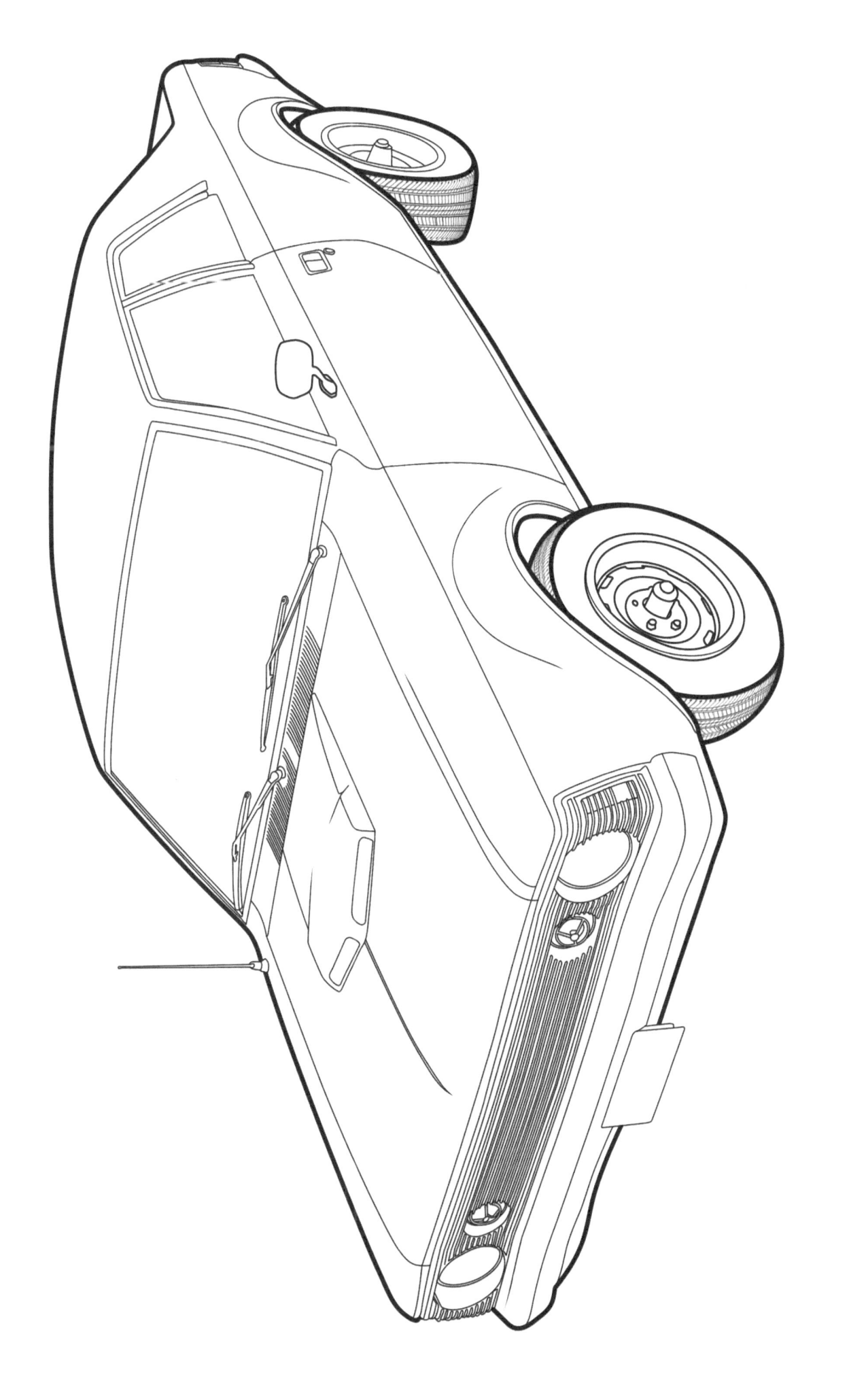

Shelby Cobra 427 Super Snake 1967

Shelby Mustang GT500 KR 1968

De Tomaso Pantera GT5 1973

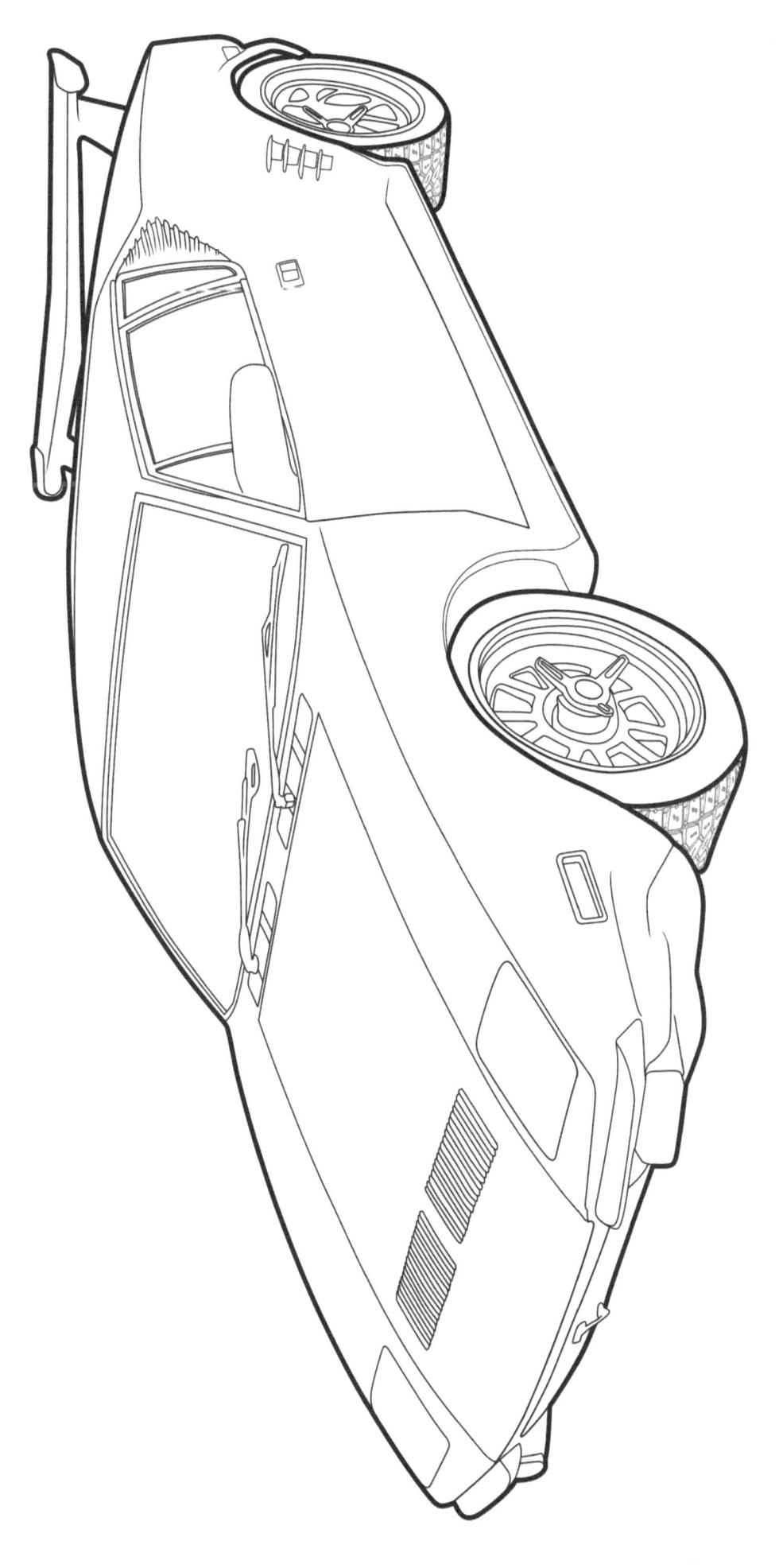

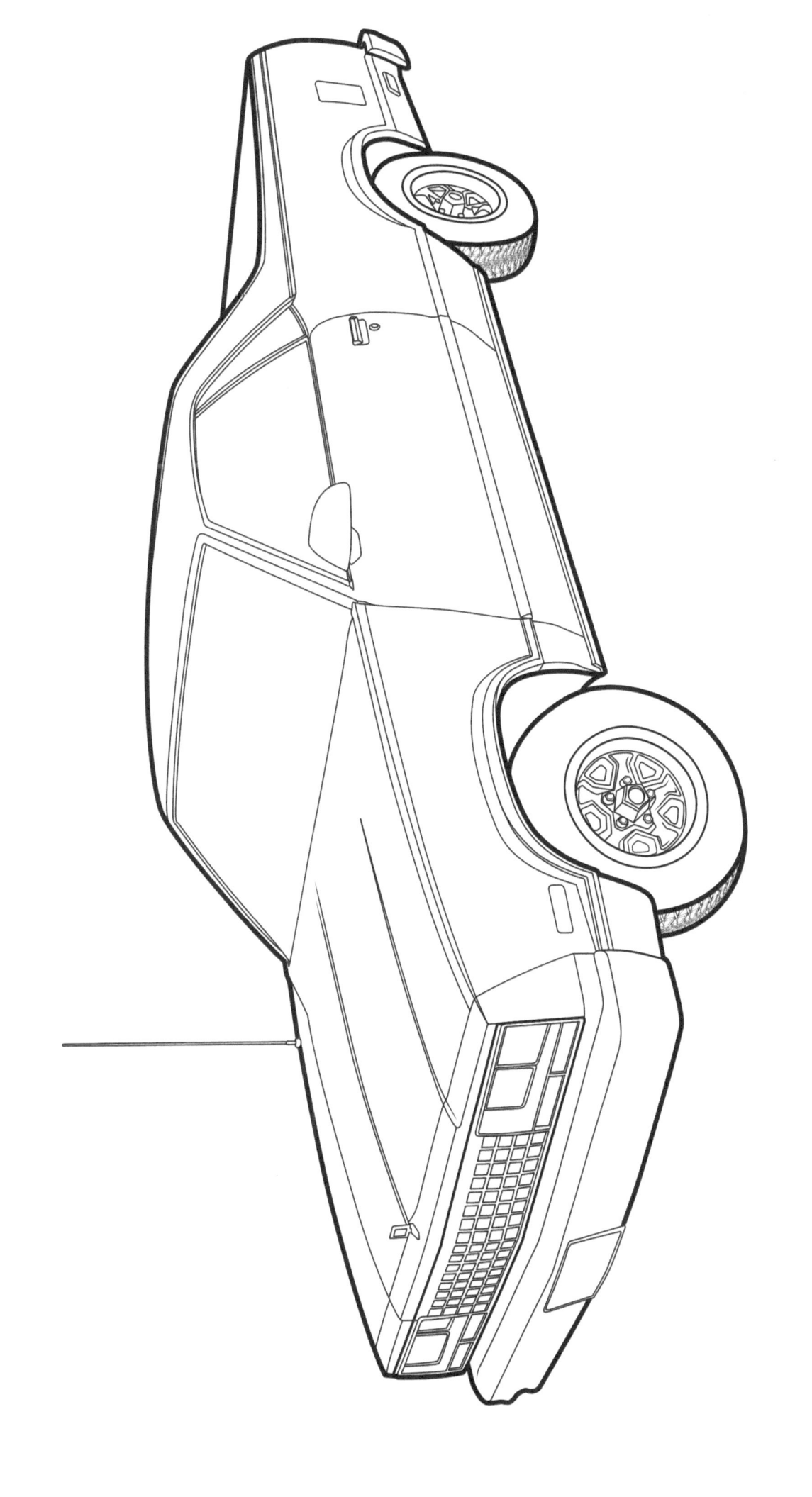

GMC Caballero Diablo Truck 1978

Lamborghini Countach 1979

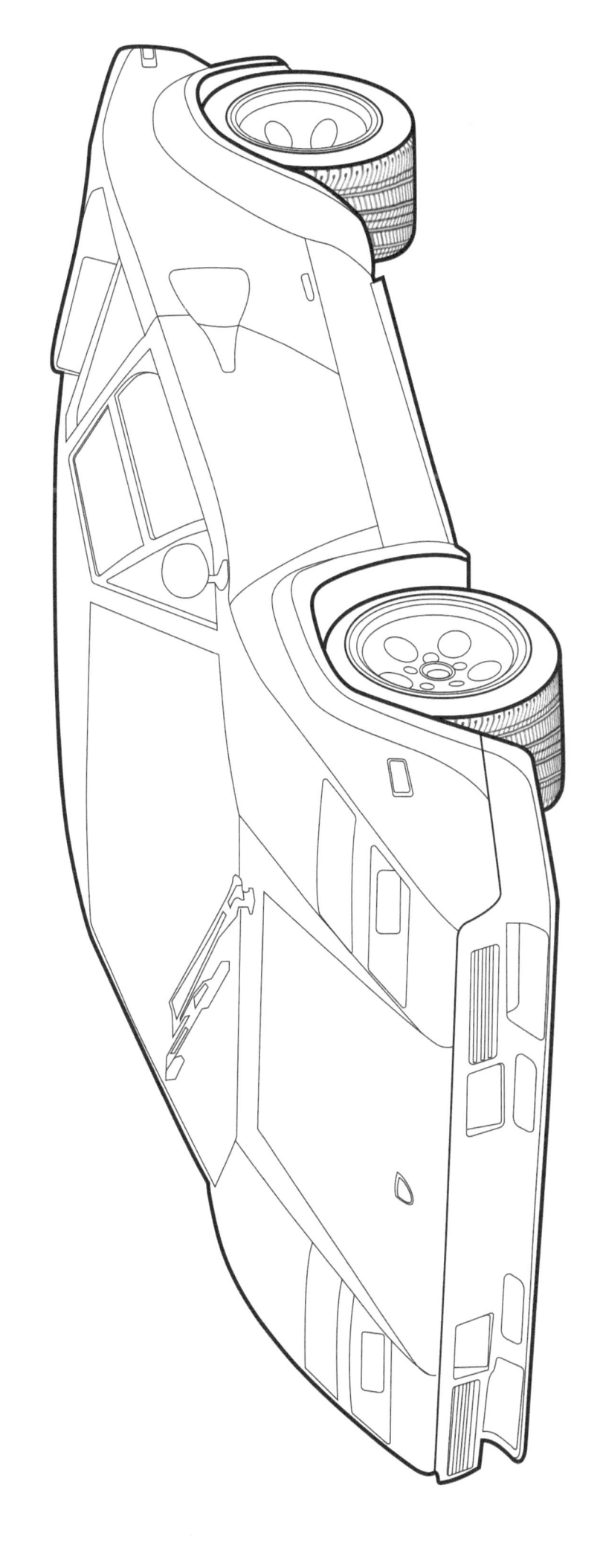

Thank you for purchasing our book

Please don't forget to leave a review as

this helps us to improve

the quality for you

scan the QR code for convenience

Made in United States
Troutdale, OR
01/30/2024

17320522R00058